ELITES

SPECIAL OPERATIVES IN SKIRMISH COMBAT

CONTENTS

INTRODUCTION

In Warhammer 40,000: Kill Team, every warrior is a hero in their own desperate war story. Yet there are those combatants whose heroism – or indeed the diabolical opposite – sets them above comrade and enemy alike. These elite operatives are death incarnate, and their arrival spells doom for the foe.

Warhammer 40,000: Kill Team is a fast-paced skirmish game that depicts battles between bands of hard-bitten warriors. Though kill teams may number only a handful of individuals, they are sent to achieve victory where entire armies cannot. Assassination, sabotage, couriering vital messages through active war zones – these and hundreds of similar missions fall to the kill teams. However, when the stakes are highest and the objectives are most crucial, those teams will comprise the most elite specialists that the warlords of the Warhammer 40,000 galaxy can deploy.

Highly trained stealth agents drive deep into enemy territory, veiled by technology or sorcery. Massively armoured Terminators or Ork Meganobz blast their way down foe-packed tunnels to tear the heart from the enemy's defences. Towering Custodian Guard form a gilded shield before Imperial commanders and allow none to harm their wards. Asuryani Aspect Warriors launch pre-emptive raids that will save or damn worlds. *Kill Team: Elites* allows you to include such paragons of war in your games of Kill Team.

The following pages contain exciting background about these hand-picked groups of killers, the natures of the missions on which they are sent and the myriad ways they bring death to their foes. From famous maximum-force kill teams and their conquests, to the distinctive methods they employ in battle and the ferociously lethal weapons they bring to bear, there is a wealth of information in this book to inspire your own collections and narrative games of Kill Team.

You will also find rules for an array of new kill team operatives that can be included for almost every faction, along with their matched play points costs and wargear profiles. Additionally, *Kill Team: Elites* contains rules for a new faction, the Adeptus Custodes, as well as background tables to provide you with names, character quirks and a backstory for your Custodian Guard kill team. There are also a range of new Tactics for every faction in Kill Team that will expand your strategic options, rules for sub-factions such as different Space Marine Chapters, and a number of new missions to really put your warriors through their paces.

A kill team of Blightlord Terminators battle the Terminator elite of the Ultramarines Chapter amidst the tumbled ruins of the Macrobasilica Imperialis on Asmordean V.

WAR HEROES

'The sharpest blade cuts the
deepest. Rest assured, there is no
keener blade in all the Emperor's
wide realm than the warriors of
the Adeptus Custodes.'

- Captain-General Trajann Valoris

THE CHOSEN FEW

Across the horrific battlefields of the 41st Millennium stride powerful bands of ultra-elite warriors who possess the might to break entire armies. Deployed as specialist kill teams at crucial strategic junctures, their efforts can determine the fate of star systems, and turn the tide in interplanetary campaigns.

In every war there comes a time when a commander must call upon the finest combatants they have at their disposal. Perhaps these are berserk killers, sent in to spearhead a breakthrough offensive that absolutely must shatter the enemy lines. Perhaps they are a carefully husbanded reserve of heavily armed and armoured warriors who can be relied upon to stop just such a headlong assault in its tracks and – in doing so – break the enemy's strength.

In other cases these forces may be expert assassins against whom no armed guards, sealed bulkheads or complex defences are sufficient. They may be talented sappers who can bring down the mightiest fortress, terrifying masters of the hit-and-run raid, or specialist operatives such as zealous witch-finders, steely-eyed abduction squads or immovable bodyguards who will lay down their lives to defend their charge.

Whatever the case, if a commander is wise then a single such kill team can be employed to strike blows that entire armies could not. Perhaps a rogue planetary governor has led their world in an open revolt against the Imperium, in the process seizing control of a heavily fortified planet and brainwashing all of its loyal defenders to their corrupt cause. It might cost months of grinding warfare and millions of lives for a conventional army to crush the rebellion. Instead, the pinpoint deployment of an elite kill team can see the governor's head on a spike over their fortress gates by daybreak, and the rebellion hurled into disarray. A sprawling army of anonymous guards might be infiltrated or broken apart by a cunning foe. Instead, a single brotherhood of dedicated and supremely skilled protectors will ensure that their precious ward makes it through enemy territory unharmed, or the strategic site they patrol remains inviolate no matter the enemy's efforts.

In these ways and many more, such kill teams prove themselves to be worth hundreds of lesser warriors. Possessing operational autonomy and superhuman skills, boasting the most potent wargear their species' armouries can provide, they bestride the battlefield like demigods and crush all before them. And should two such rarefied warbands meet upon the field of battle? Then all present bear witness to a conflict unlike any other, a blistering display of martial prowess and destructive fury that spawns legends and horror stories both.

WEAPONS OF WAR

Whether they be hulking Ork Nobz, stalwart Space Marine Terminators or T'au Crisis Battlesuit pilots, the warriors of specialist kill teams have access to some of the most incredible technologies seen in the 41st Millennium. Energised blades that can cut through adamantium as though it were parchment; suits of servo-assisted or jet-propelled fully enclosed combat armour proof against the vacuum of space; high-spec sniper rifles whose sights can see through bulkheads and jamming fields alike to pinpoint the prey beyond; the list goes on. Whatever equipment such a team is issued, their commander can rest assured they will draw upon every advantage it affords them to complete their missions with swift efficiency.

Key to the success of many kill teams are those technologies or talents that allow them to bypass the greater mass of foes and strike where and when they

WINTERFANG'S RIMEGUARD

Beoric Winterfang is the most respected of Wolf Lord Krom Dragongaze's Wolf Guard. He leads the Rimeguard, a band of Terminator-armoured Space Marines who strike like the icy wrath of a Fenrisian storm. These champions have deployed as kill team operatives on many occasions, and from Alaric Prime to the Gurdanesh Rift they have carved out mighty sagas for themselves.

Beoric is stoic and immovable as the Fang itself. He is the ice to his Wolf Lord's fire, reining in Krom's famous temper with cool-headed counsel. For all this, Winterfang is a ferocious fighter who tears through his enemy with savage economy of effort, and wades unflinching through the heaviest fire to achieve his goals.

Beoric is supported in battle by the grizzled slayer and inveterate pessimist Olaf the Dour, the battle-scarred and irascible Wulfrik Stormsmite with his heavy flamer, hot-headed and belligerent Senvi Frostheart, and Joten Sourtongue, the hero of Karbor Heights. By flame and fury, by bolt and blade, this highly experienced pack have completed countless vital missions on behalf of Wolf Lord Krom.

need to. In the case of some warriors, this may simply be down to an exceptional level of skill in remaining unseen and undetected, such as that evinced by the Striking Scorpion Aspect Warriors of the Asuryani. In other cases, it may present more as an inherent talent or esoteric ability. Tyranid Raveners, for example, can tunnel through soil, bedrock, and even ferrocrete foundations in order to ambush their prey. Drukhari Mandrakes are more terrifying still. The ghastly creatures slip from shadowed corners, squeezing like spiders through impossibly small gaps or even lunging through mirror surfaces to drag their jagged blades across their victims' throats.

Other warriors, most notably the Terminators of the Adeptus Astartes and Heretic Astartes, make use of arcane technologies to launch their attacks. Stepping into the crackling hearts of teleportation shrines aboard orbiting spacecraft, these heavily armoured warriors vanish from reality in squalls of unnatural energies and travel instantaneously through the perilous realm of the warp. They then explode into existence in the very midst of their shocked foes. The slaughter that follows such a risky and audacious deployment is bloody in the extreme.

HEROES AND VILLAINS

Mission-critical kill teams – those with tasks that absolutely cannot fail lest an entire war zone collapse – are often led into the fray by exceptional individuals, paragons and exemplars of their species whose abilities as strategists, leaders and fighters place them head and shoulders above their comrades and their enemies alike. Phobos-armoured Primaris Space Marine officers lead targeted insertion raids to strike down rival commanders, or to steal strategic secrets from the very minds of their enemies. Genestealer Cult Kelermorphs whirl and spin through the maelstrom of combat, pistols barking again and again as they hammer their quarry with deadly accurate salvoes. Dark Apostles of the Heretic Astartes storm into the fray, smashing their victims to a bloody pulp with their tainted croziuses even as they bellow corrupting verses of heretical scripture that inspire their allies and send their enemies fleeing in abject terror.

Then there are those individuals so adept in the arts of murder that their names spread in hushed whispers across entire galactic sectors. Boss Snikrot, the dreaded 'Green Ghost' of the Armageddon jungles and the most accomplished Ork Kommando in the galaxy; Sly Marbo, the Catachan one-man army whose hollow stare is feared by his commanders almost as much as his terrifying affinity with guns, blades and explosive devices is feared by his enemies; Darkstrider, the most sinister and controversial of all the T'au Empire's military heroes, a shadowy figure who leads his Pathfinder Teams in ever more audacious and desperate raids against the enemy's greatest strongholds with scant regard for the commands or codes of his superiors. Such figures may fight alone or they may lead, but whatever the case, their presence in a combat zone is sure to spell doom for their foes.

A kill team of Blood Angels Terminators storms through the twisted chambers of the Space Hulk *Sin of Damnation*, blasting a path through hordes of Tyranid Genestealers to reach their vital objective.

DREAD THEATRES

Specialised kill teams are often deployed when a mission's environs or hazards are considered beyond the capabilities of all other warriors. Space Marine Terminator Squads, for example, are the favoured option for Imperial commanders looking to clear out the monstrous ghost ships known as space hulks. These hellish agglomerations of wrecked spacecraft are melded by the foul energies of the warp into floating derelicts the size of small planets. Space hulks are characterised by mile upon mile of twisting corridors, claustrophobic chambers and warped bulkheads behind which may lurk all manner of deadly xenos or Chaos-tainted threats.

Entire sections of a space hulk may lie open to the ferocious cold of the void. Others are so saturated with radiation that even Space Marine power armour would not long shield its wearer from a horrible death. With blind corners, half-seen crawl spaces and areas of absolute darkness common, predatory aliens can strike so swiftly and suddenly that only warriors clad in hulking Tactical Dreadnought armour have any hope of surviving long enough to open fire and purge their assailants.

A monstrous Black Legion Terminator storms into battle, smashing aside all in his path.

Space hulks are far from the only battlefields inimical to life. Some are riddled with unnatural plagues or contaminated with the biological fallout of planetary virus bombardment. The Blightlord Terminators of the Death Guard stride through such contamination zones with clotted snorts of contempt. They wade through liquefied corpse-mulch and kick down quarantine bulkheads, sure in the knowledge that the virulent blessings of the Plague God Nurgle render them immune to all other forms of infection.

'Don't be preposterous, Sergeant. There is absolutely no way that the enemy could reach us in here. Mark my words, we're as well protected as the Golden Throne itself!'

*- Last words of Captain Ultyn
(slain by Mandrakes)*

The golden-armoured demigods of the Adeptus Custodes could not be further removed from the revolting Blightlords, but they share their impervious nature. In the Custodes' case this superhuman resilience stems from the incredible genetic alchemy involved in their creation. Every cell of their bodies resounds with an echo of the Emperor's divine might. So blessed, the Custodian Guard may pass un-helmed through the void of space when need demands, stride uncaring through firestorms and acid blizzards, and withstand the malign touch of Chaos corruption. This renders their kill teams able to pursue their enemies no matter where they flee.

There are as many examples of such combat-zone specialisms as there are types of battlefield to be fought across. Hulking Bullgryns stomp relentlessly through blistering salvoes that would annihilate platoons of lesser soldiery, the enemy's shots ricocheting from slabshields and tank-track armour in the moments before the Bullgryns unleash their bone-shattering charge. Triarch Praetorians engage their enemies across lethal ice floes or battlefields running with lava, their metallic hides impervious to the extreme conditions even as their gravity-repelling displacement packs enable them to circumvent the battlefield's hazards and use them to trap their victims. The Paladins of the Grey Knights storm into battle amidst the sanity-destroying horrors of full-blown daemonic incursions, their spiritual purity and exceptional mental conditioning allowing them to endure sights that would drive lesser minds to madness.

Whether it be a Genestealer Cults Sanctus squirming through derelict pipes to find the perfect vantage point, Asuryani Wraithguard striding like ghosts across an airless moonscape, or Primaris Suppressors descending on grav-chutes to trap the foe behind their own barricades, these elite operatives master every aspect of even the most dangerous battlefield and turn it to their advantage.

FACTIONAL EXPERTISE

There are countless sub-factions and warrior cultures dotted throughout the galaxy, and a wise commander takes note of the particular ways of war that their elite operatives practise. In battles between such heroic warbands victory balances upon a razor's edge, and the officer who best exploits their warriors' skills is likely to win the day.

The Chapters of the Adeptus Astartes exemplify this trend. The Ultramarines and their many successor Chapters maintain a doctrine of strategic balance and versatility. However, the scions of many of the other Primarchs lean more towards particular skill-sets, operational specialisms and – often archaic – warrior traditions. The White Scars and their successors, for example, possess the Great Khan's predilection for lightning warfare, striking swift and hard before vanishing again to attack from another angle. By comparison, the Imperial Fists and all those who share their gene-seed make a virtue of belligerence, demonstrating courage and stoicism far beyond that expected even of the Adeptus Astartes. The Space Wolves form gung-ho warrior packs who seek glory in sagas and demonstrate daring that borders on foolhardiness, while the Iron Hands fight with the cold indifference of battle-cogitators and can slice their victims to pieces with their perfectly calculated overlapping fields of fire.

Other races, too, exhibit such variations. Drukhari who hail from the Kabal of the Poisoned Tongue exhibit a capacity for arrogance that sees them stay in the fight no matter the odds, the better to prove their superiority. Kabalite Warriors in the employ of the Obsidian Rose may wield the finest weaponry imaginable, while those who fight for the Kabal of the Flayed Skull have a reputation for being so vicious that even their malevolent kin are wary of them.

Amongst the Necrons, different dynasties prize particular traits and show tactical eccentricities. Every thought and deed of a Sautekh Dynasty Lychguard is governed by a fragment of their master's hyper-logical strategic protocols, meaning that together they can close around their enemies like an inescapable steel fist. By comparison, those belonging to the Nihilakh Dynasty

are governed by algorithms so advanced their reactions could be mistaken for precognition, while those hailing from the Nephrekh Dynasty bear shining exoskeletons of molten solar gold whose fiery light blinds their foes.

The Tyranids also display distinctive traits that mark out the weapon-beasts of different hive fleets. The organisms of Hive Fleet Behemoth rampage through their prey driven by a monstrous hunger for biomass that can never be sated. Those of Hive Fleet Leviathan are far subtler, demonstrating frightening levels of adaptation to the environmental conditions and enemies they are likely to face during an invasion. The creatures of Hive Fleet Gorgon exude lethal toxins that can swiftly overcome even the most stalwart enemies, while the swarms of Hive Fleet Jormungandr burrow under the battlefield until entire regions are riddled with hive-like tunnel networks, and the enemy has no idea where their attackers will emerge from next.

Whatever their nature, when elite-operative kill teams are sent into an engagement that suits their particular talents, they unleash such focused carnage that their assaults can seem prescient to their enemies. In a few unsettling cases, this may even be the truth…

TOOFRIPPA'S KREW

Kaptin Rezgil Toofrippa is amongst the most wily and dangerous Ork Flash Gitz to curse the space-lanes of the 41st Millennium. Leading the bunch of cut-throat murderers and bully-boy braggarts that comprise his Krew, Toofrippa wanders the stars in search of gainful employ from any Warboss sufficiently shifty or rich – or both – to afford his exorbitant price.

Though their hiring fee would fund the construction of a Stompa, Toofrippa's Krew are worth it. The Kaptin himself is as devious as they come, always ready to sabotage his enemies' assets – or those of his rivals, given half the chance – and packing phenomenal firepower in the form of his monstrous snazzgun. The rest of Toofrippa's Krew are scarcely less formidable than their boss. Deddskull Drom is so resilient as to appear all but unkillable, while Grobber Drog loves blowing things up the way angry squigs love biting people's faces off. The hulking Tragg Rokkfist is no stranger to bashing his enemies' brains in, preferring to use his snazzgun 'up close and persnul' as a bludgeon. Meanwhile, the loud-mouthed newcomer Brakka is so determined to earn his place on the Krew that he will take any risk in battle, no matter how madcap. Thus far he has survived, however, leading some to claim he has the luck of Mork and others to suggest he's 'just cheatin''.

RULES

'There is a code to every battle,
a set of rules, be they formally
acknowledged or wholly unwritten,
to which combatants conform.
Understanding the rules by
which you fight is the first step
to victory.'

*- Tactica Imperialis Advanced
Operations Strategic Scripture*

ELITE OPERATIVES

This book contains rules to expand your games of Warhammer 40,000: Kill Team. There's a new Commander specialism, rules for bringing Reserves onto the battlefield, new Tactics and new datasheets for most Factions, plus Sub-faction rules and new missions to challenge your reinforced kill team.

LEGENDARY HUNTER SPECIALISTS

Legendary Hunter is a new Commander specialism unique to some of the stealthiest and most lethal warriors of the Warhammer 40,000 galaxy. Such individuals are ideally suited to the skirmish-style warfare of Kill Team games, and as such they have access to a new set of skills and Tactics that reflect their almost supernatural ability in such engagements.

ADDITIONAL RULES

The Standard Deployment and Variable Battle Length rules from *Kill Team: Commanders* have been included here for ease of reference. Reserves is a new mission rule that allows you to keep warriors back, ready for them to pounce at the opportune moment by dropping from the skies or launching devastating ambushes.

SUB-FACTIONS

Kill Team: Elites introduces an exciting new set of rules – Sub-factions. Now your chosen Space Marine Chapter, Asuryani Craftworld, Necron Dynasty and more will have an impact on your battles, adding even more narrative depth and tactical variables to your games, and providing further inspiration for kill team creation.

NEW TACTICS, DATASHEETS AND FACTION

On the following pages you'll find new Tactics, collected and updated Tactics and new datasheets, including for Commanders, for most of the Factions in Kill Team, as well as a new Faction: the Adeptus Custodes. You can use all of these rules in your games of Kill Team as described in the *Kill Team Core Manual*. Note that to include Commanders in your games of Kill Team and to use their Aura Tactics, you will need a copy of *Kill Team: Commanders*. If you have more than one version of a Tactic (e.g. one printed in this book and another printed on a card), you can choose which one to use, but cannot use both versions in the same game.

The datasheets on the pages that follow use a mix of familiar and new wargear. Where wargear is new, you will find its rules on the relevant datasheet (for a Commander) or in the reference section for your Faction (for all other models). Where wargear has already been presented in the *Kill Team Core Manual*, its rules are not repeated in this book, so if a piece of wargear does not appear on a datasheet or in the reference section for your Faction, refer to the *Kill Team Core Manual* for its rules. However, you must use the points values given in this book for datasheets from this book: these are found below the relevant datasheet (for a Commander) or in the reference section for your Faction (for all other models). Datasheets from other Kill Team publications are not affected.

Amongst ferrocrete barricades and smouldering ruins, Ork Flash Gitz pour salvoes of fire into the Blightlord Terminators that advance relentlessly upon them.

LEGENDARY HUNTER SPECIALISTS

When a Commander has the Legendary Hunter specialism, their datasheet will state what level they are (they are always at that level and cannot gain experience). The Commander has the abilities stated at that level and all lower levels (so a Commander who is a Level 3 Legendary Hunter has the Hard Case, Sudden Ambush and Stealthy Hunter abilities). You also have access to the Legendary Hunter Tactics for your Commander's level and all lower levels. Legendary Hunter specialists cannot have Commander Traits.

LEGENDARY HUNTER LEVEL 1

Hard Case: Ignore the penalty to this model's hit rolls from flesh wounds it has suffered.

LEVEL 2

Sudden Ambush: When you set up this model from Reserve, set them up anywhere on the battlefield that is more than 5" away from any enemy models.

LEVEL 3

Stealthy Hunter: When an opponent makes a hit roll or Injury roll for a shooting attack that targets this model, and this model is obscured, that hit roll or Injury roll suffers an additional -1 modifier.

LEVEL 4

Like Fighting a Shadow: Once per battle, at the start of any Movement phase, if there are no enemy models within 6" of this model (other than shaken models) and this model is not shaken, you may remove this model from the battlefield and place them in Reserve.

NINE LIVES

Level 1 Legendary Hunter Tactic

Use this Tactic when your opponent makes an Injury roll for a Legendary Hunter specialist from your kill team. They must subtract 1 from each of the dice rolled.

1 COMMAND POINT

FIGHTING WITH THE LEGEND

Level 2 Legendary Hunter Tactic

Use this Tactic at the beginning of the Morale phase if there is a Legendary Hunter of Level 2 or higher that is not shaken on the battlefield. That model and friendly models within 2" of them automatically pass any Nerve tests in this phase.

1 COMMAND POINT

LEGENDARY SKILL

Level 3 Legendary Hunter Tactic

Use this Tactic when you choose a Legendary Hunter of Level 3 or higher to attack in the Shooting phase or Fight phase. You can re-roll failed hit and wound rolls for that model until the end of the phase.

2 COMMAND POINTS

ADDITIONAL RULES

These pages contain two commonly used mission rules, and also introduce the rules for Reserves to your games of Warhammer 40,000: Kill Team. The Reserves rules allow you to bring models from your kill team onto the battlefield after the mission has started.

STANDARD DEPLOYMENT

Some Kill Team missions say that they use the Standard Deployment rules. Where a mission states this, use the following rules when deploying your kill teams.

The players each roll 2D6. The highest scorer has the greatest strategic advantage in this mission, the next highest has the second greatest advantage and so on. Any players who roll the same result roll their dice again to determine which of them has a greater advantage. The players then take it in turn, in the order of greatest to least advantage, to choose their deployment zone.

The players then take it in turn, in the order of least to greatest advantage, to deploy one model from their kill team. Models must be set up wholly in their own deployment zone. Once all players have set up one model, they do so again in the same order, and so on. If a player runs out of models to set up, skip them. Once the players have set up all of their models, deployment ends and the first battle round begins.

VARIABLE BATTLE LENGTH

Some Kill Team missions last for a variable number of battle rounds (in some cases, they may last for a variable number of battle rounds unless some other condition is met, e.g. there is only one unbroken kill team on the battlefield). Where a mission states that it uses the Variable Battle Length rules, use the following rules to determine when the battle ends. Each mission that uses these rules tells you which player makes the roll.

If the battle does not end otherwise, at the end of battle round 4, roll a D6. The battle continues on a 3+, otherwise the battle ends. If the battle does not end otherwise, at the end of battle round 5, roll a D6. This time the battle continues on a 4+, otherwise the battle ends. The battle automatically ends at the end of battle round 6.

RESERVES

The rules found here can be used in any games of Kill Team, with the exception of missions that use the Ultra-close Confines rules.

SETTING UP IN RESERVE

During deployment, instead of setting up a model on the battlefield as described by the mission, you can set that model up in Reserve. You can do this with up to half of the models in your kill team, but if you are using a Battle-forged kill team, the total points cost of any models you set up in Reserve can be no greater than half of your kill team's Force.

SETTING UP FROM RESERVE

A model that is set up in Reserve can be set up on the battlefield at the end of any Movement phase. At the end of the phase, if a player has any models in Reserve, they can decide to set up one or more of them on the battlefield. If more than one player has any models in Reserve, the players take it in turn to set up all of the models they wish to (including using any Reserve Tactics they wish to use, as described below), in the order determined in the Initiative phase.

Players do not have to set up any models from Reserve if they do not wish to, but if any models are still in Reserve at the end of the third battle round, they are considered to be out of action. When a model is set up from Reserve, it must be set up on the battlefield more than 5" from any enemy models and within 1" of the edge of the battlefield. It must also be wholly within your deployment zone, where the mission provides a deployment zone. Note that the restrictions described in Reinforcements in the *Kill Team Core Manual* apply to models set up in this way.

RESERVE TACTICS

Some Tactics alter how models arrive from Reserve. When players use these Tactics as part of their models arriving from Reserve, they do so in the sequence described above and by following the instructions on the Tactic. Note that the restrictions described in Reinforcements in the *Kill Team Core Manual* apply to models set up in this way, unless stated otherwise.

The following Tactic can be used by any player with at least one model in Reserve.

OUTFLANK

Tactic

Use this Tactic at the end of the Movement phase. Choose a model from your kill team that was set up in Reserve and set them up within 1" of the edge of the battlefield and more than 5" away from any enemy models.

1 COMMAND POINT

Amidst the tumbled ruins of an Imperial hive city, the howling warriors of Winterfang's Rimeguard meet a suppurating band of Blightlord Terminators in brutal close-quarters combat.

SUB-FACTIONS

This section presents the rules for using Sub-factions in your games of Kill Team. The armies of the galaxy are infinitely diverse, and even amongst the genetically engineered warriors of the Adeptus Astartes there are variations that lead to differing strengths and ways of making war.

Each set of Sub-factions tells you which Faction keyword it applies to (e.g. **ADEPTUS ASTARTES**). When you add a model with that Faction keyword to your kill team or command roster, you can choose for it to be drawn from a Sub-faction of your choice from those listed in that Faction's section within this book (so when you add a model with the **ADEPTUS ASTARTES** keyword to your command roster, you could choose for it be drawn from the Ultramarines, for example). When you choose a Sub-faction for a model in this way, make a note of that on the model's datacard. Its Sub-faction is treated as an additional keyword that the model has, so a model drawn from the Ultramarines has the **ULTRAMARINES** keyword.

If your kill team is Battle-forged and all models in your kill team are drawn from the same Sub-faction, models in the kill team gain a Sub-faction ability as described in that Faction's section. The Sub-faction ability gained depends upon the Sub-faction you chose, as described in that Faction's section. For example, if you chose the Ultramarines Chapter for your **ADEPTUS ASTARTES** kill team, the models in your kill team gain the Codex Discipline Chapter Tactic. In addition to gaining a Sub-faction ability for the models in your kill team, you also gain access to Tactics that are unique to that Sub-faction. For example, if you chose the Ultramarines Chapter, you can use Ultramarines Tactics.

Unless stated otherwise, if your kill team is drawn from a Sub-faction that does not have an associated Sub-faction ability, choose a Sub-faction from that Faction's section that best describes its character and fighting style.

Primaris Space Marine Intercessors of the Imperial Fists Chapter lay down a blistering hail of fire, their kill team advancing relentlessly upon their objective regardless of the odds stacked against them.

CHAPTER TACTICS

The Sub-factions for models with the **ADEPTUS ASTARTES** Faction keyword are called Chapters, and their Sub-faction abilities are called Chapter Tactics. If your kill team is Battle-forged and all models in your kill team are drawn from the same Chapter, models in the kill team gain the Chapter Tactic described below, and you can use that Chapter's Tactics.

If your kill team is drawn from a Chapter that does not have an associated Chapter Tactic, use the Chapter Tactic of its founding Chapter. For example, Crimson Fists are a successor Chapter of the Imperial Fists, so should use the Chapter Tactic of the Imperial Fists. If you are unsure of a Chapter's founding Chapter, either consult the background sections of our books or choose a Chapter Tactic from those below that best describes its character and fighting style. In some cases, the Chapter a model is drawn from may change the model's wargear options – where this is the case, this will be mentioned on the model's datasheet.

DARK ANGELS: GRIM RESOLVE

The stalwart descendants of the Lion are renowned for their unshakeable resolve, enduring tenacity and strict fire discipline in battle.

You can re-roll hit rolls of 1 for shooting attacks made by models in your kill team (including when firing Overwatch) that have not moved in this battle round. In addition, you can re-roll the dice to determine whether or not your kill team is broken in the Morale phase.

WHITE SCARS: LIGHTNING ASSAULT

The White Scars are true masters of the hunt. Theirs is the primal fury of the storm, the scent of prey upon the wind. None can escape their righteous justice.

When a model in your kill team Advances, add an additional 2" to the distance it can move. In addition, if a model in your kill team started the Movement phase within 1" of an enemy model, but when you pick it to move there are no enemy models within 1", that model can make a charge attempt instead of Falling Back or remaining stationary.

SPACE WOLVES: HUNTERS UNLEASHED

The Space Wolves train their whole lives for the moment when battle is joined. After a long hunt tensed for the kill, they spring forward to devastating effect.

In any battle round in which a model in your kill team charged, was charged or made a pile-in move granted by the Heroic Intervention Commander Tactic, add 1 to hit rolls for attacks made by that model in the Fight phase. In addition, you can use the Heroic Intervention Commander Tactic if there are any enemy models within 6" (rather than 3") of your Commander, and when you do so they can make a pile-in move of 6" (rather than 3").

IMPERIAL FISTS: SIEGE MASTERS

None are as well versed in siege warfare as the Imperial Fists. No fortress world is safe from their pinpoint bombardments and disciplined fusillades of bolter fire.

Models in your kill team do not suffer the penalty to Injury rolls for the target of their attacks being obscured and within 1" of a model or piece of terrain that is between the two models.

BLOOD ANGELS: THE RED THIRST

Though they strive to restrain it at every turn, the murderous ferocity of the Blood Angels simmers just beneath the surface of their thoughts. In battle this rage can be used as a weapon, lending fearsome strength to the Blood Angels' blows.

In any battle round in which a model in your kill team charged, was charged or made a pile-in move granted by the Heroic Intervention Tactic, add 1 to wound rolls for attacks made by that model in the Fight phase.

Iron Hands: The Flesh is Weak

The Iron Hands seek transcendence through the replacement of their mortal flesh with cybernetics and metal augments. Such extensive modification renders them extremely difficult to kill.

Roll a dice each time a model in your kill team loses a wound. On a 6, the damage is ignored and the model does not lose a wound. If a model already has a similar ability, choose which effect applies, and re-roll 1s when making these rolls.

Ultramarines: Codex Discipline

The sons of Guilliman hold the tenets of the Codex Astartes as sacrosanct. In the fury of combat its wisdom guides them as they outmanoeuvre and overpower the foe with lethal precision.

Add 1 to the Leadership characteristic of all models in your kill team. In addition, models in your kill team can still shoot in a battle round in which they Retreated or Fell Back, but if they do so a 6 is always required for a successful hit roll, irrespective of the firing model's Ballistic Skill or any modifiers.

Salamanders: Master Artisans

The Salamanders are peerless craftsmen, capable of forging weapons of astounding quality and lethal power from the furnaces of Nocturne.

You can re-roll a single failed hit roll and a single failed wound roll in each phase, as long as the attack was made by a model in your kill team.

Raven Guard: Shadow Masters

From the shadows strike the Raven Guard, emerging with dizzying speed to gut the foe before they can react.

Models in your kill team are considered to be obscured to enemy models that target them if they are more than 12" away from those models.

Black Templars: Righteous Zeal

True believers in the Imperial Creed, the Black Templars wish for nothing more than to slaughter the heretic and the xenos in the name of the God-Emperor.

You can re-roll charge rolls for models in your kill team.

REGIMENTAL DOCTRINES

The Sub-factions for models with the **Astra Militarum** Faction keyword are called regiments, and their Sub-faction abilities are called Regimental Doctrines. If your kill team is Battle-forged and all models in your kill team are drawn from the same regiment, models in the kill team gain the Regimental Doctrine described opposite, and you can use that regiment's Tactics.

MILITARUM TEMPESTUS

Models with the **Militarum Tempestus** keyword cannot be drawn from a regiment. However, their presence in your kill team does not prevent you using a Regimental Doctrine, as long as the models in the kill team that can be drawn from a regiment are all drawn from the same regiment. Note, however, that models with the **Militarum Tempestus** keyword can never themselves benefit from a Regimental Doctrine, unless every model (other than Advisors and Auxilla, see opposite) in that kill team has the **Militarum Tempestus** keyword (in which case you will use the Storm Troopers Regimental Doctrine).

ADVISORS AND AUXILLA

Models with the following keywords cannot be drawn from a regiment. However, their presence in your kill team does not prevent you using a Regimental Doctrine, as long as the models in the kill team that can be drawn from a regiment are all drawn from the same regiment. Note, however, that models with the following keywords can never themselves benefit from a Regimental Doctrine.

- **Aeronautica Imperialis**
- **Militarum Auxilla**
- **Officio Prefectus**
- **Scholastica Psykana**

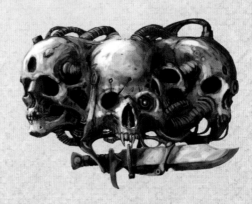

Cadian: Born Soldiers

Cadians are raised from birth to fight the Imperium's endless wars. Decades of rigorous firing drills have forged them into expert sharp-shooters.

Re-roll unmodified hit rolls of 1 in the Shooting phase for models in your kill team if they have not moved in this battle round. If a model in your kill team is issued the 'Take Aim!' order and it has not moved in this battle round, re-roll all failed hit rolls for that model until the end of the phase instead.

Catachan: Brutal Strength

In the deadly jungles of Catachan, only the strongest survive. The sons and daughters of this death world are ferocious warriors, taller and more powerful than typical humans.

Add 1 to the Strength characteristic of models in your kill team. In addition, add 1 to the Leadership characteristic of models in your kill team if they are within 6" of a friendly Catachan Officer.

Valhallan: Grim Demeanour

Possessed of a grim fatalism regarding the prospect of death, Valhallan Ice Warriors will march unflinchingly into the most hellish of firestorms.

When you take a Nerve test for a model in your kill team, roll a D3 (instead of a D6).

Vostroyan: Heirloom Weapons

Each and every Vostroyan weapon is lovingly hand-crafted and engraved with intricate ornamental detail. These are no artisanal trinkets, however, as victims of their deadly accurate firepower will attest.

Models in your kill team do not suffer the penalty to hit rolls for their attacks that target enemy models at long range.

Armageddon: Industrial Efficiency

To the Steel Legions of Armageddon, the pitiless mathematics of industrialised slaughter have become a grim fact of life. One by one, their foes are butchered with dispassionate efficiency.

Models in your kill team firing Rapid Fire weapons double the number of attacks they make if all of their targets are within 18" (instead of half the weapon's Range characteristic).

Tallarn: Swift as the Wind

Masters of the lightning ambush, Tallarn warriors strike with overwhelming force before swiftly fading into the wilderness as if they were never there at all.

Models in your kill team can shoot in the Shooting phase even if they Advanced in the same battle round (with the exception of Heavy weapons). In addition, these models do not suffer the penalty to their hit rolls for shooting Assault weapons during a battle round in which they Advanced.

Militarum Tempestus: Storm Troopers

The warriors of the Militarum Tempestus are the best of the best, merciless killers trained to obliterate their foes in a pinpoint fusillade of hot-shot las-rounds.

If a model in your kill team targets an enemy model that is within range and not at long range when making a shooting attack, it can make an extra shot with the same weapon, at the same target, for each unmodified hit roll of 6.

Mordian: Parade Drill

Mordian regiments are proud, unyielding soldiers. They fight and die facing the enemy, standing tall in ordered ranks and unleashing a devastating fusillade of las-fire.

If the base of a model in your kill team is touching the base of at least two other friendly Mordian models, add 1 to that model's Leadership characteristic, and when that model fires Overwatch they successfully hit on a roll of 5 or 6.

FORGE WORLD DOGMA

The Sub-factions for models with the **Adeptus Mechanicus** Faction keyword are called forge worlds, and their Sub-faction abilities are called Forge World Dogmas. If your kill team is Battle-forged and all models in your kill team are drawn from the same forge world, models in the kill team gain the Forge World Dogma described below, and you can use that forge world's Tactics.

Mars: Glory to the Omnissiah

In all the Cult Mechanicus, there are no forge worlds more holy or more blessed than Mars. The favour of the Machine God can be seen in the powerful optimisation granted by every static-ridden psalm incanted by his most faithful followers.

Each time you randomly determine which Canticle of the Omnissiah (see the *Kill Team Core Manual*) is being canted, roll two dice instead of one. Models in your kill team receive the benefit of both results, instead of just the result of the first dice (if a duplicate is rolled, no additional Canticle is canted this turn).

Graia: Refusal to Yield

Steely minded tenacity and the refusal to retreat are more than just character traits of those who serve Graia. Indeed, such qualities are hard-wired into all who bear the forge world's symbol.

Roll a dice each time a model in your kill team is reduced to 0 wounds. On a roll of 6, they are restored to 1 wound remaining. In addition, models in your kill team pass Nerve tests on an unmodified roll of 6 (as well as an unmodified roll of 1). However, models in your kill team cannot Retreat or Fall Back unless there is a **Commander** from your kill team on the battlefield.

Metalica: Relentless March

Those of Forge World Metalica seek nothing less than to completely obliterate their foes and to re-order the galaxy according to their own dictates. They will let nothing sway their appointed task.

Models in your kill team can shoot Rapid Fire weapons as if they were Assault weapons in the Shooting phase of a battle round in which they Advanced (e.g. a Rapid Fire 1 weapon would be used as if it were an Assault 1 weapon). In addition, these models do not suffer the penalty to their hit rolls for shooting Assault weapons during a battle round in which they Advanced.

Lucius: The Solar Blessing

Lucius is renowned for its craftsmanship and its unique solar-blessed ores. Those clad in such raiment consider themselves armoured by their faith in the Omnissiah.

When making saving throws for models in your kill team, treat enemy attacks with an Armour Penetration characteristic of -1 as having an Armour Penetration of 0 instead.

Agripinaa: Staunch Defenders

Battle-hardened by constant clashes with the horrors that issue out of the Eye of Terror, those from Forge World Agripinaa have learned the lessons of defensive warfare well.

When a model in your kill team fires Overwatch, they successfully hit on a roll of 5 or 6.

Stygies VIII: Shroud Protocols

When the armies of Stygies VIII march to war, they do so beneath stealth screen projectors and target-befouling apparatus. That the Tech-Priests of this forge world deny owning such technology only reinforces their untrustworthy reputation.

Models in your kill team are considered to be obscured to enemy models that target them if they are more than 12" away from those models.

Ryza: Red in Cog and Claw

Tech-Priests of Ryza point to aggressive combat doctrines and zealous training protocols to explain the exceptional hand-to-hand prowess of their troops. Sceptics, however, counter that such designs do not explain why Ryza troops seem to revel in close-quarters violence.

You can re-roll wound rolls of 1 in the Fight phase for attacks made by models in your kill team.

LEGION TRAITS

The Sub-factions for models with the **Heretic Astartes** Faction keyword are called Legions, and their Sub-faction abilities are called Legion Traits. If your kill team is Battle-forged and all models in your kill team are drawn from the same Legion, models in the kill team gain the Legion Trait described below, and you can use that Legion's Tactics. If your kill team is drawn from a Renegade Chapter or does not otherwise have an associated Legion Trait, use the Renegade Chapters Legion Trait.

CHAOS CULTISTS

Models with the **Chaos Cultist** keyword cannot be drawn from a Legion. However, their presence in your kill team does not prevent you using a Legion Trait, as long as the models in the kill team that can be drawn from a Legion are all drawn from the same Legion. Note, however, that models with the **Chaos Cultist** keyword can never themselves benefit from a Legion Trait.

EMPEROR'S CHILDREN: FLAWLESS PERFECTION

Inured to everyday sensations by lifetimes of indulgence, the Emperor's Children find stimulation only in excess, be it shocking acts of violence or gratuitous displays of martial prowess.

Only models with the **Slaanesh** keyword can be drawn from this Legion. If a model in your kill team is within 1" of an enemy model at the beginning of the Fight phase, the model in your kill team is considered to have charged.

IRON WARRIORS: SIEGE LORDS

Cold-hearted killers whose only faith is in their wargear, the Iron Warriors have perfected siege warfare, and are able to gouge out even the most entrenched foes.

Models in your kill team do not suffer the penalty to Injury rolls for the target of their attacks being obscured and within 1" of a model or piece of terrain that is between the two models.

NIGHT LORDS: TERROR TACTICS

The Night Lords revel in fear and mayhem, and will take apart an opposing army piecemeal, isolating the weakest enemies so that their confused cries can be savoured.

When an opponent takes a Nerve test for a model from their kill team, they must add 1 to the test for each of your models (other than shaken models) that is within 3" of that model.

WORLD EATERS: BUTCHER'S NAILS

Angron's sons hurl themselves towards their foe, intent on tearing them apart in a brutal whirlwind of violence.

Only models with the **Khorne** keyword can be drawn from this Legion. You can make one additional attack in the Fight phase with a model in your kill team if it charged, was charged or made a pile-in move granted by the Heroic Intervention Commander Tactic in that battle round.

BLACK LEGION: BLACK CRUSADERS

Inexorable and unflinching, the Black Legion exemplify the threat posed by the Heretic Astartes, emerging from the Eye of Terror for the sole purpose of erasing the Imperium from the galaxy.

Add 1 to the Leadership characteristic of models in your kill team. In addition, models in your kill team can shoot Rapid Fire weapons as if they were Assault weapons in the Shooting phase of a battle round in which they Advanced (e.g. a Rapid Fire 1 weapon would be used as if it were an Assault 1 weapon).

WORD BEARERS: PROFANE ZEAL

The Word Bearers march to war for the glory of the Chaos pantheon, stirred into a rapturous state of fanaticism by blasphemous catechisms and the dark promises of the Ruinous Powers.

You can re-roll failed Nerve tests for models in your kill team.

ALPHA LEGION: HIDDEN IN PLAIN SIGHT

The warriors of the Alpha Legion are masters of duplicity, able to mislead and misdirect even the most vigilant of enemies before delivering the killing blow.

Models in your kill team are considered to be obscured to enemy models that target them if they are more than 12" away from those models.

RENEGADE CHAPTERS: DARK RAIDERS

Freed from the constraints of the Imperium, Renegade Astartes indulge their enhanced capacity for violence.

You can re-roll charge rolls for models in your kill team.

CRAFTWORLD ATTRIBUTES

The Sub-factions for models with the **Asuryani** Faction keyword are called craftworlds, and their Sub-faction abilities are called Craftworld Attributes. If your kill team is Battle-forged and all models in your kill team are drawn from the same craftworld, models in the kill team gain the Craftworld Attribute described below, and you can use that craftworld's Tactics.

ULTHWÉ: FORESIGHT OF THE DAMNED

All Aeldari are psychically attuned, but none more so than those of Ulthwé. Perhaps tainted by their long proximity to the Eye of Terror, their intuition borders well into prescience.

Roll a dice each time a model in your kill team loses a wound. On a 6, the damage is ignored and the model does not lose a wound. If a model already has a similar ability, choose which effect applies, and re-roll 1s when making these rolls.

SAIM-HANN: WILD HOST

Each member of a Saim-Hann Wild Host longs to be the first into the fight, the one to win all the glory; nothing stands between them and their quarry.

You can re-roll charge rolls for models in your kill team.

ALAITOC: FIELDCRAFT

Through a combination of stealth, superior scouting reports and peerless camouflage, Alaitoc warriors are able to obscure themselves upon the battlefield.

Models in your kill team are considered to be obscured to enemy models that target them if they are more than 12" away from those models.

BIEL-TAN: SWORDWIND

Biel-Tan warhosts are famed for the indomitable spirit of their Aspect Warriors, as well as for the prodigious storms of shuriken fire they unleash upon the foe.

Add 1 to the Leadership characteristic of **Aspect Warriors** in your kill team. In addition, you can re-roll hit rolls of 1 for shuriken weapons used by models in your kill team. A shuriken weapon is any weapon profile whose name includes the word 'shuriken' (e.g. shuriken pistol, Avenger shuriken catapult etc.). The ranged profile of a scorpion's claw is also a shuriken weapon.

IYANDEN: STOIC ENDURANCE

The tenacity of those from Iyanden is the stuff of legends. Their craftworld has suffered much, yet the spirits of both its living and dead remain unbowed.

When you take a Nerve test for a model in your kill team, roll a D3 (instead of a D6).

DRUKHARI OBSESSIONS

The Sub-factions for models with the **Drukhari** Faction keyword are called Kabals, Wych Cults and Haemonculus Covens, and their Sub-faction abilities are called Drukhari Obsessions. A model's keywords indicate whether it can be drawn from a **Kabal**, **Wych Cult** or **Haemonculus Coven**. If your kill team is Battle-forged and all models in your kill team are drawn from the same Kabal, Wych Cult or Haemonculus Coven, models in the kill team gain the Drukhari Obsession described below, and you can use that Sub-faction's Tactics.

If your kill team is drawn from a Kabal, Wych Cult or Haemonculus Coven that does not have an associated Drukhari Obsession, choose a Drukhari Obsession for the appropriate type of Sub-faction from those listed below that best describes its character and fighting style.

EXISTING DATASHEETS

Kabalite Warriors and Archons gain the **Kabal** keyword. Wyches and Succubi gain the **Wych Cult** keyword. Haemonculi gain the **Haemonculus Coven** keyword.

BLADES FOR HIRE

Drukhari models that do not have the **Kabal**, **Wych Cult** or **Haemonculus Coven** keywords cannot be drawn from a Kabal, Wych Cult or Haemonculus Coven, but can be included in a Drukhari kill team without preventing other models in that kill team from gaining a Drukhari Obsession. Note, however, that these models can never themselves benefit from a Drukhari Obsession.

KABAL OF THE BLACK HEART: THIRST FOR POWER

Though by far the largest and most influential Kabal, the Black Heart has been taught by Vect to never be satisfied, and to rapaciously pursue ever more power.

Models in your kill team treat the current battle round as being 1 higher than it actually is when determining what bonuses they gain from their Power From Pain ability (see the *Kill Team Core Manual*). Models in your kill team that do not have the Power From Pain ability instead gain the Inured to Suffering bonus (see Power From Pain in the *Kill Team Core Manual*).

KABAL OF THE FLAYED SKULL: INESCAPABLE SLAYERS

The Kabalites of the Flayed Skull excel in swift and shockingly violent raids, using their speed and manoeuvrability to harry the most elusive targets.

Models in your kill team do not suffer the penalties to hit rolls for the target of their attacks being obscured or because of intervening terrain.

KABAL OF THE POISONED TONGUE: THE SERPENT'S KISS

The toxin crafters of the Kabal of the Poisoned Tongue tailor their venoms to the targets of a raid, ensuring they will have the most gruesome effect on the victims' physiologies.

Re-roll wound rolls of 1 made for melee weapons and poisoned weapons used by models in your kill team. For the purposes of this obsession, a poisoned weapon is any weapon that wounds on a particular roll (e.g. on a 4+).

KABAL OF THE OBSIDIAN ROSE: FLAWLESS WORKMANSHIP

Every weapon produced in the workshops of the Kabal of the Obsidian Rose is a masterpiece, equal in accuracy and lethality to the finest armaments of other Kabals.

Models in your kill team do not suffer the penalty to hit rolls for their attacks that target enemy models at long range.

CULT OF STRIFE: THE SPECTACLE OF MURDER

Whether enthralling spectators in the arena or slaughtering their way through an enemy army, the Cult of Strife have developed a penchant for bombastically violent opening manoeuvres.

You can make one additional attack in the Fight phase with a model in your kill team if it charged, was charged or made a pile-in move granted by the Heroic Intervention Commander Tactic in that battle round.

CULT OF THE CURSED BLADE: ONLY THE STRONG WILL THRIVE

There is no place for frailties amongst the Cult of the Cursed Blade, for they teach that weakness exists only to be exploited by the strong. Those Wyches who survive in the Cult's arena are the physical embodiment of this philosophy.

Increase the Strength characteristic of models from in your kill team by 1. In addition, when you take a Nerve test for a model in your kill team, subtract 1 from the result.

CULT OF THE RED GRIEF: SPEED OF THE KILL

Wyches of the Cult of the Red Grief revel in high-speed murder, and there is fierce competition amongst their ranks as to who can butcher their victims the quickest.

You can re-roll charge rolls for models in your kill team.

THE PROPHETS OF FLESH: CONNOISSEURS OF PAIN

The Prophets of Flesh have modified their own bodies and those of their servants to an extraordinary extent – so much so that few weapons their enemies bring to bear against them can inflict damage greater than that they have already endured.

Models in your kill team with the Insensible to Pain ability have an invulnerable save of 4+ (rather than 5+).

THE DARK CREED: DISTILLERS OF FEAR

The Coven of the Dark Creed has perfected every method of inducing terror, to the extent that their mere presence fills the minds of their enemies with nightmarish dread.

When an opponent takes a Nerve test for a model from their kill team, they must add 1 to the test for each of your models (other than shaken models) that is within 3" of that model.

COVEN OF TWELVE: BUTCHERS OF FLESH

The practice of internecine assassinations that exists amongst the Coven of Twelve ensures that weapons and wits are kept razor-sharp at all times, and only those members who are master flesh-carvers survive long.

Improve the Armour Penetration characteristic of all melee weapons used by a model in your kill team by 1. For example, an Armour Penetration characteristic of 0 becomes -1, an Armour Penetration characteristic of -1 becomes -2, and so on.

MASQUE FORMS

The Sub-factions for models with the **Harlequins** Faction keyword are called masques, and their Sub-faction abilities are called Masque Forms. If your kill team is Battle-forged and all models in your kill team are drawn from the same masque, models in the kill team gain the Masque Form described below, and you can use that masque's Tactics.

MIDNIGHT SORROW: THE ART OF DEATH

The warrior acrobats of the Midnight Sorrow move with exceptional purpose and singular dedication upon the field of battle.

Models in your kill team can move an additional D6" when they Fall Back. In addition, they can consolidate up to 6".

VEILED PATH: RIDDLE-SMITHS

Harlequins of the Masque of the Veiled Path are tricksters without peer, and to meet them in battle is to encounter hallucination and misdirection from every quarter.

At the start of each Fight phase roll two dice and discard the highest result. Until the end of the phase, each time an opponent targets a model in your kill team and makes a hit roll that, before modifiers, exactly matches your dice result, that hit roll fails.

FROZEN STARS: HYSTERICAL FURY

The Masque of Frozen Stars fight with frenetic glee, slaying in a mirthful frenzy that is terrifying to behold.

You can make one additional attack in the Fight phase with a model in your kill team if it charged, was charged or made a pile-in move granted by the Heroic Intervention Commander Tactic in that battle round.

SOARING SPITE: SERPENT'S BROOD

The Masque of the Soaring Spite strike like the Weaver Serpents of Aeldari myth, swift and sudden.

Models in your kill team treat all Pistol weapons they are equipped with as Assault 1 weapons during a battle round in which they Advanced. In addition, these models do not suffer the penalty to their hit rolls for shooting Assault weapons during a battle round in which they Advanced.

DREAMING SHADOW: SOMBRE SENTINELS

The Harlequins of the Dreaming Shadow are steeped in the grotesque and the ghastly; their only fear is that their eternal watch might falter or fail.

When you take a Nerve test for a model in your kill team, subtract 1 from the result. In addition, when a model in your kill team is taken out of action, roll a D6 before removing that model: on a 4+, that model can make a shooting attack with one weapon as if it were the Shooting phase, or make a single attack as if it were the Fight phase.

SILENT SHROUD: DANCE OF NIGHTMARES MADE FLESH

To fight the Silent Shroud is to do battle with your own worst fears, magnified into a silent storm that smothers sanity and suffocates rational thought until all that remains is animalistic terror.

Subtract 1 from the Leadership characteristic of enemy models while they are within 3" of any models in your kill team. In addition, whenever an opponent takes a Nerve test for a model that is within 3" of any models in your kill team, they must roll two dice and discard the lowest result.

DYNASTIC CODES

The Sub-factions for models with the **Necrons** Faction keyword are called dynasties, and their Sub-faction abilities are called Dynastic Codes. If your kill team is Battle-forged and all models in your kill team are drawn from the same dynasty, models in the kill team gain the Dynastic Code described below, and you can use that dynasty's Tactics.

DYNASTIC AGENTS

Triarch Praetorians cannot be drawn from a dynasty, but can be included in a Necrons kill team without preventing other models in that kill team from gaining a Dynastic Code. Note, however, that Triarch Praetorians can never themselves benefit from a Dynastic Code.

Sautekh: Relentless Advance

Nothing can halt the inexorable march of the Sautekh. These disdainful conquerors will stop at nothing to retake their ancient domain, obliterating any who dare defy them in a storm of death and destruction.

Models in your kill team can shoot ranged weapons as if they were Assault weapons in the Shooting phase of a battle round in which they Advanced (e.g. a Rapid Fire 1 weapon would be used as if it were an Assault 1 weapon).

Mephrit: Solar Fury

The Mephrit have harnessed the power of captive suns to power their weapons. This raging solar energy can sear through even the thickest armour with ease.

If a model in your kill team targets an enemy model that is within range and not at long range when making a shooting attack, improve the Armour Penetration characteristic of that weapon's attack by 1 (i.e. an Armour Penetration characteristic of '0' becomes '-1', an Armour Penetration characteristic of '-1' becomes '-2', etc.).

Novokh: Awakened by Murder

The crimson hosts of Novokh remember well the sacred rites of blooding performed by their warriors in the ancient times. The dynasty's proud martial heritage awakens a spark of violent pride within its legions, lending power and ferocity to their attacks.

You can re-roll failed hit rolls in the Fight phase for attacks made by a model in your kill team if it charged, was charged or made a pile-in move granted by the Heroic Intervention Commander Tactic in that battle round.

Nihilakh: Aggressively Territorial

Regal and arrogant, the warriors of this proud dynasty will not give a single inch to their foes. They stand their ground defiantly, unleashing a formidably accurate hail of fire that cleanses the stain of the lesser races from their rightful lands.

Re-roll unmodified hit rolls of 1 in the Shooting phase for models in your kill team if they have not moved in this battle round.

Nephrekh: Translocation Beams

The bodies of the Nephrekh are crafted from metagold. This rare and wondrous alloy allows them to transform into beams of pure light in order to teleport across open ground and even phase through solid matter.

If a model in your kill team Advances, you can re-roll the D6 to determine the increase to that model's Move characteristic. In addition, if a model in your kill team Advances, it can move across models and terrain as if they were not there.

CLAN KULTURS

The Sub-factions for models with the **Orks** Faction keyword are called clans, and their Sub-faction abilities are called Clan Kulturs. If your kill team is Battle-forged and all models in your kill team are drawn from the same clan, models in the kill team gain the Clan Kultur described below, and you can use that clan's Tactics.

GUNZ FOR HIRE

Flash Gitz can be included in an Ork kill team without preventing other models in that kill team from gaining a Clan Kultur. Note, however, that **Flash Gitz** can never themselves benefit from any Clan Kultur unless every model in that kill team (other than **Gretchin** – see Grots, below) is drawn from the Freebooterz.

GROTS

Gretchin cannot be drawn from a clan, but can be included in an Orks kill team without preventing other models in that kill team from gaining a Clan Kultur. Note, however, that **Gretchin** can never themselves benefit from any Clan Kultur.

GOFFS: NO MUKKIN' ABOUT

Goff Orks are the biggest, meanest and most ferocious of their kind. Once they get stuck into hand-to-hand combat, the Goffs quickly overwhelm their enemies by dint of sheer violent ferocity.

Each time you make an unmodified hit roll of 6 for an attack with a melee weapon made by a model in your kill team, immediately make an additional hit roll against the same target using the same weapon. These additional hit rolls cannot themselves generate any further hit rolls.

BAD MOONS: ARMED TO DA TEEF

Bad Moons are ostentatious show-offs, whose predilection for toting the biggest, loudest and shiniest shootas means that they can typically lay down a storm of dakka that eclipses the firepower of any other clan.

Re-roll hit rolls of 1 for attacks made by models in your kill team in the Shooting phase.

EVIL SUNZ: RED ONES GO FASTA

The Evil Sunz are firm believers in the old Ork adage 'red ones go fasta', and so the Orks of this clan make sure to daub their vehicles and themselves bright red. Bizarrely, the practice actually seems to work.

Add 1 to the Move characteristic of models in your kill team, and add 1 to Advance and charge rolls made for them. In addition, these models do not suffer the penalty to their hit rolls for shooting Assault weapons during a battle round in which they Advanced.

DEATHSKULLS: LUCKY BLUE GITZ

All Orks believe blue to be a lucky colour, but the notoriously superstitious Deathskulls are fervent in that belief. The clan's members are in the habit of daubing themselves liberally with blue warpaint.

Models in your kill team have a 6+ invulnerable save, unless they already have an invulnerable save. In addition, you can re-roll a single failed hit roll and a single failed wound roll in each phase, as long as the attack was made by a model in your kill team.

SNAKEBITES: DA OLD WAYS

Snakebites are seen as a bit backwards to the other Ork clans. However, their refusal to rely upon 'newfangled rubbish' and their habit of allowing themselves to be bitten by venomous serpents to prove their toughness makes them remarkably resilient warriors.

Roll a dice each time a model in your kill team loses a wound. On a 6 the wound is not lost. If a model already has a similar ability, choose which effect applies, and re-roll 1s when making these rolls.

BLOOD AXES: TAKTIKS

The Blood Axes are seen as untrustworthy by other Orks, but they couldn't care less; they possess an instinctive grasp of battlefield strategy that – while still undeniably Orky in its application – allows them to surprise even the most seasoned enemy commanders.

Models in your kill team are considered to be obscured to enemy models that target them if they are more than 18" away from those models. In addition, models in your kill team can shoot even if they Fell Back in the same battle round.

FREEBOOTERZ: COMPETITIVE STREAK

There's something a little off about most Freebooterz. These mercenary loot-hounds are just that bit more mean-spirited, vicious and sneaky, and substantially more competitive than their fellow greenskins.

Add 1 to hit rolls for attacks made by models in your kill team for each other model in your kill team that has taken an enemy model out of action with an attack in this phase.

SEPT TENETS

The Sub-factions for models with the **T'au Empire** Faction keyword are called septs, and their Sub-faction abilities are called Sept Tenets. If your kill team is Battle-forged and all models in your kill team are drawn from the same sept, models in the kill team gain the Sept Tenet described below, and you can use that sept's Tactics.

KROOT

Kroot models cannot be drawn from a sept, but can be included in a T'au Empire kill team without preventing other models in that kill team from gaining a Sept Tenet. Note, however, that **Kroot** models can never themselves benefit from any Sept Tenet.

T'au Sept: Coordinated Fire Arcs

The rigorously drilled Fire Warriors of T'au Sept utilise overlapping fields of fire to envelop charging enemies in a kill-storm of searing pulse energy.

When a model in your kill team uses their For the Greater Good ability, or when they fire Overwatch whilst they are within 6" of a friendly model, they successfully hit on a roll of 5 or 6.

Vior'la Sept: Strike Fast

The Commanders of Vior'la harness their warriors' fiery temperaments by embracing a highly mobile and aggressive form of warfare, taking the fight to the heart of the enemy.

Models in your kill team can shoot Rapid Fire weapons as if they were Assault weapons in the Shooting phase of a battle round in which they Advanced (e.g. a Rapid Fire 1 weapon would be used as if it were an Assault 1 weapon). In addition, these models do not suffer the penalty to their hit rolls for shooting Assault weapons during a battle round in which they Advanced.

Bork'an Sept: Superior Craftsmanship

From Bork'an Sept's renowned applied science divisions come the most advanced and ingenious weapon prototypes, field-tested by elite contingents of Fire caste soldiers.

Models in your kill team do not suffer the penalty to hit rolls for their attacks that target enemy models at long range.

Dal'yth Sept: Adaptive Camouflage

The T'au of Dal'yth prize victory at any cost, and have mastered the art of sudden ambushes and elaborate traps. They utilise adaptive camouflage fields to elude and disorient their foes.

If a model in your kill team does not move in the Movement phase, for the remainder of the battle round it is considered to be obscured to enemy models that target it.

Sa'cea Sept: Calm Discipline

The Fire Warriors of the densely populated Sa'cea Sept train extensively for the close-range hell of city combat, learning the vital importance of fire discipline and combined arms.

Add 1 to the Leadership characteristic of models in your kill team. In addition, you can re-roll hit rolls of 1 for shooting attacks made by models in your kill team.

Farsight Enclaves: Devastating Counter-strike

Commander O'Shovah's mastery of Mont'ka has bled into the martial culture of the Farsight Enclaves. Its warriors are experts in the deadly art of engaging the enemy in close confines.

Re-roll hit and wound rolls of 1 for shooting attacks made by models in your kill team that target an enemy model that is within 6" of the firing model.

HIVE FLEET ADAPTATIONS

The Sub-factions for models with the **Tyranids** Faction keyword are called hive fleets, and their Sub-faction abilities are called Hive Fleet Adaptations. If your kill team is Battle-forged and all models in your kill team are drawn from the same hive fleet, models in the kill team gain the Hive Fleet Adaptation described below, and you can use that hive fleet's Tactics.

If you are using a splinter fleet rather than a hive fleet, use the Hive Fleet Adaptation of its parent hive fleet. For example, the Court of the Nephilim King is a splinter fleet of Hive Fleet Behemoth, so should use the Behemoth Hive Fleet Adaptation. If you are unsure of a splinter fleet's parent hive fleet, either consult the background sections of our books or choose an adaptation from those below that best describes its character and fighting style.

BEHEMOTH: HYPER-AGGRESSION

Driven by a frenzied hunger, Hive Fleet Behemoth unleashes the full might of its swarms in an overwhelming frontal assault.

You can re-roll charge rolls for models in your kill team.

KRAKEN: QUESTING TENDRILS

The Kraken harries and unbalances its foes with lightning-fast flanking attacks, before encircling them for the final, bloody massacre.

When a model in your kill team Advances, roll three D6 instead of one and pick the highest to add to the Move characteristic of that model for that Movement phase. In addition, if a model in your kill team started the Movement phase within 1" of an enemy model, but when you pick it to move there are no enemy models within 1", that model can make a charge attempt instead of Falling Back or remaining stationary.

LEVIATHAN: SYNAPTIC IMPERATIVE

Hive Fleet Leviathan's synaptic network is so strong that its organisms can be compelled by the Hive Mind to fight in spite of injuries that should have crippled or slain them outright.

Roll a D6 each time a model in your kill team loses a wound whilst it is within 6" of a friendly **Synapse** model. On a 6, the damage is ignored and the model does not lose a wound. In addition, models in your kill team that are within 6" of a friendly **Synapse** model do not suffer the penalty to their hit rolls from one flesh wound they have suffered.

GORGON: ADAPTIVE TOXINS

The toxins produced by Hive Fleet Gorgon's swarm-creatures adapt with terrifying speed to any foe, agonising and ravaging the bodies of their unfortunate victims.

You can re-roll wound rolls of 1 in the Fight phase for attacks made by models in your kill team.

JORMUNGANDR: TUNNEL NETWORKS

The warrior-organisms of Hive Fleet Jormungandr attack from subterranean tunnels, making them extremely difficult to target until it is far too late.

Models in your kill team (other than models that can **Fly**) are considered to be obscured to enemy models that target them. If the model Advances or charges, however, it loses this benefit until the end of the battle round.

HYDRA: SWARMING INSTINCTS

Hive Fleet Hydra's super-swarms overwhelm their prey with sheer weight of numbers, drowning them in a tide of chitin, flesh and slashing claws.

You can re-roll hit rolls in the Fight phase for attacks made by models in your kill team that target an enemy model that is within 1" of another model in from your kill team.

KRONOS: BIO-BARRAGE

Hive Fleet Kronos obliterates its foes at range by unleashing devastating barrages of bio-plasma and living missiles.

Re-roll unmodified hit rolls of 1 in the Shooting phase for models in your kill team if they have not moved in this battle round.

CULT CREEDS

The Sub-factions for models with the **Genestealer Cults** Faction keyword are called cults, and their Sub-faction abilities are called Cult Creeds. If your kill team is Battle-forged and all models in your kill team are drawn from the same cult, models in the kill team gain the Cult Creed described below, and you can use that cult's Tactics (e.g. if all models in your kill team are drawn from the Cult of the Four-armed Emperor, those models gain the Subterranean Ambushers Cult Creed, and you can use Cult of the Four-armed Emperor Tactics).

XENOS PHYSIOLOGY

Genestealer models cannot be drawn from a cult. However, their presence in your kill team does not prevent you using a Cult Creed, as long as the models in the kill team that can be drawn from a cult are all drawn from the same cult. Note, however, that models with the **Genestealer** keyword can never themselves benefit from a Cult Creed.

CULT OF THE FOUR-ARMED EMPEROR: SUBTERRANEAN AMBUSHERS

The Cult of the Four-armed Emperor hails from a mining dynasty. It specialises in launching surprise assaults from the subterranean realms of the Imperium.

Add 1 to Cult Ambush rolls made for models in your kill team.

THE TWISTED HELIX: EXPERIMENTAL SUBJECTS

The bio-alchemists of the Twisted Helix seek to perfect their hybridised creations by blending the strength of the Genestealer with human stock in inventive new ways.

Add 1 to the Strength characteristic of models in your kill team. In addition, when a model in your kill team Advances add an additional 2" to the distance it can move.

THE RUSTED CLAW: NOMADIC SURVIVALISTS

The Rusted Claw believe they need only to endure to secure total victory. The scruffy and weather-beaten appearance of these nihilists belies a hidden stamina.

When making saving throws for models in your kill team, treat enemy attacks with an Armour Penetration characteristic of -1 as having an Armour Penetration of 0 instead.

THE HIVECULT: DISCIPLINED MILITANTS

The Hivecult recruits its converts from military organisations and criminal underworlds. It values firepower highly, and knows how best to use it.

When you take a Nerve test for a model in your kill team, roll a D3 (instead of a D6). In addition, models in your kill team can shoot in a battle round in which they Retreated or Fell Back, but if they do so a 6 is always required for a successful hit roll, irrespective of the firing model's Ballistic Skill or any modifiers.

THE BLADED COG: CYBORGISED HYBRIDS

Often hailing from forge worlds, cultists of the Bladed Cog blend man, machine and alien into disgusting hybrid anatomies that they see as perfect organisms.

Models in your kill team have a 6+ invulnerable save. Models in your kill team that already have an invulnerable save instead improve their invulnerable save by 1 (to a maximum of 3+). In addition, models in your kill team do not suffer the penalty to their hit rolls for moving and shooting Heavy weapons.

THE PAUPER PRINCES: DEVOTED ZEALOTS

The frothing fanatics of the Pauper Princes believe that martyrdom is the finest of acts. They fight with a religious frenzy when their fellows are threatened.

You can re-roll failed hit rolls in the Fight phase for attacks made by a model in your kill team if it charged, was charged or made a pile-in move granted by the Heroic Intervention Commander Tactic in that battle round.

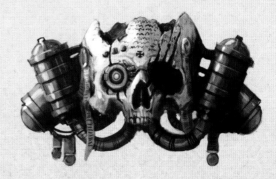

ADEPTUS ASTARTES

The Adeptus Astartes, known more commonly as the Space Marines, specialise in lightning assaults, precision raids and targeted offensives designed to annihilate the enemy's ability to coordinate or fight back. Their ranks include numerous brotherhoods of highly skilled warriors perfectly suited to such operations.

The Angels of Death, the Emperor's Finest, the Imperium's Greatest Hope – all these names and more have been applied to the mighty Adeptus Astartes. These Space Marines are post-human champions one and all, formed into Chapters of a thousand heroic warriors apiece. Each Space Marine Chapter is a self-contained army capable of conquering entire worlds, supported by its own armouries, vehicles and spacecraft and boasting its own formidable warrior culture. What the Space Marines lack in numbers, they more than make up for in sheer martial might.

Every Space Marine is a genetically enhanced super soldier whose speed, strength, resilience, intelligence, courage and combat capabilities are nothing short of breathtaking. They are psycho-indoctrinated and rigorously trained to face the most terrifying or seemingly impossible strategic challenges. They are armed and equipped with the finest wargear the Imperium can provide. In short, the Space Marines are the equal of any of the monstrous threats that assail the Emperor's Realm.

Space Marines can live for centuries, providing they are not slain in battle. Their veteran warriors accrue an incredible wealth of experience from their lives of constant war. Squads of Sternguard and Vanguard Veterans are often deployed in kill teams where their martial wisdom and peerless ability can make the difference between victory and defeat. Sternguard Veterans are superlative marksmen whose skill with a wide variety of ranged weapons makes short work of even the toughest targets. By comparison, Vanguard Veterans are masterful assault specialists. They often use jump packs to bound across the battlefield in rocket-assisted leaps, and take the fight to the foe with crackling power fists and roaring chainswords.

Other Space Marine Veterans – not to mention the Chapter's heroic leaders – go to war clad in suits of indomitable Terminator armour. Effectively transformed into walking tanks, these warriors can teleport into battle, shrug off firepower that would devastate entire squads of lesser warriors, and unleash weaponry that would seem more at home on a mechanised combat walker. Under the right conditions, a handful of Terminators can slaughter an army's worth of enemies, and their might as kill team operatives cannot be overstated.

In recent years, a new breed of Space Marine – the Primaris brethren – have joined the ranks of the Adeptus Astartes. Whether bolstering existing Chapters or forming entirely new ones, their heightened physical capabilities and specialised wargear have afforded the Space Marines a number of new strategic options that have rendered them more versatile and deadly than ever. The Primaris battle-brothers of the Vanguard detachments are clad in sleek Phobos-pattern armour and wield formidable weaponry. They specialise in dismantling the enemy war machine, slaying high-profile targets, spreading terror and sabotaging communications and supply lines with impunity.

ADEPTUS ASTARTES KILL TEAMS

If every model in your kill team has the ADEPTUS ASTARTES Faction keyword, you can use Adeptus Astartes Tactics.

GRAV-CHUTE DESCENT

Adeptus Astartes Tactic

Use this Tactic at the end of the Movement phase. Choose up to three models that are any combination of GRAV-CHUTE and/or REIVER models from your kill team that were set up in Reserve and set them up anywhere on the battlefield that is more than 5" away from any enemy models.

1 COMMAND POINT

JUMP PACK ASSAULT

Adeptus Astartes Tactic

Use this Tactic at the end of the Movement phase. Choose up to three JUMP PACK models from your kill team that were set up in Reserve and set them up anywhere on the battlefield that is more than 5" away from any enemy models.

1 COMMAND POINT

ANGEL OF DEATH

Adeptus Astartes Tactic

Use this Tactic after choosing a model that charged in this battle round to fight with. Add 1 to that model's Attacks characteristic for this phase.

1 COMMAND POINT

TELEPORT STRIKE

Adeptus Astartes/Deathwatch Tactic

Use this Tactic at the end of the Movement phase. Choose up to three TERMINATOR models from your kill team that were set up in Reserve and set them up anywhere on the battlefield that is more than 5" away from any enemy models.

1 COMMAND POINT

SMOKE GRENADES

Adeptus Astartes Tactic

Use this Tactic at the beginning of the Shooting phase. Choose an INFILTRATOR or a SUPPRESSOR SERGEANT from your kill team that isn't shaken. That model cannot make shooting attacks in this phase, but until the end of the phase all models within 3" of it are considered to be obscured to models that target them with shooting attacks.

1 COMMAND POINT

DEATH DENIED

Adeptus Astartes Tactic

Use this Tactic when one of your models is taken out of action. That model suffers a flesh wound instead.

2 COMMAND POINTS

CAPTAIN IN PHOBOS ARMOUR

NAME	M	WS	BS	S	T	W	A	Ld	Sv	Max
Captain in Phobos Armour	6"	2+	2+	4	4	6	5	9	3+	1

This model is armed with a master-crafted instigator bolt carbine, bolt pistol, combat knife, frag grenades and krak grenades.

WEAPON	RANGE	TYPE	S	AP	D	ABILITIES
Master-crafted instigator bolt carbine	30"	Heavy 1	4	-2	2	A model firing this weapon does not suffer the penalty to hit rolls for the target being at long range.

ABILITIES	
	And They Shall Know No Fear: You can re-roll failed Nerve tests for this model.
	Iron Halo: This model has a 4+ invulnerable save.
	Transhuman Physiology: Ignore the penalty to this model's hit rolls from one flesh wound it has suffered.
	Camo Cloak: When an opponent makes a hit roll for a shooting attack that targets this model, and this model is obscured, that hit roll suffers an additional -1 modifier.
	Concealed Position: When you set this model up during deployment, it can be set up anywhere on the battlefield that is more than 9" from any enemy deployment zone.
	Omni-scrambler: Enemy models that are set up on the battlefield from Reserve cannot be set up within 7" of this model.
SPECIALISTS	Ferocity, Fortitude, Leadership, Logistics, Melee, Shooting, Stealth, Strategist, Strength
FACTION KEYWORD	ADEPTUS ASTARTES
KEYWORDS	IMPERIUM, COMMANDER, INFANTRY, PHOBOS, PRIMARIS, CAPTAIN

RITES OF BATTLE

Adeptus Astartes Tactic
Captain in Phobos Armour
Aura Tactic

Use this Tactic at the start of the Shooting phase if your kill team includes a **PHOBOS CAPTAIN**. That model gains the following aura ability until the end of the battle round:

As long as this model is not shaken, you can re-roll hit rolls of 1 for friendly models within 6" of this model.

1 COMMAND POINT

ADEPTUS ASTARTES

MODEL	POINTS PER MODEL
Captain in Phobos Armour (Level 1)	81
Captain in Phobos Armour (Level 2)	101
Captain in Phobos Armour (Level 3)	121
Captain in Phobos Armour (Level 4)	146
WARGEAR	**POINTS PER ITEM**
Bolt pistol	0
Combat knife	0
Frag grenades	0
Krak grenades	0
Master-crafted instigator bolt carbine	0

'Enemy approach vectors confirmed. Targets entering the killbox in zero-zero-four, three, two, one... commencing Operation Scourge in the Emperor's name. Let none leave here alive.'

- Captain Hastran of the Hawk Lords

LIEUTENANT IN PHOBOS ARMOUR

NAME	M	WS	BS	S	T	W	A	Ld	Sv	Max
Lieutenant in Phobos Armour	6"	2+	3+	4	4	5	4	8	3+	1

This model is armed with a master-crafted occulus bolt carbine, bolt pistol, close combat weapon, frag grenades and krak grenades.

WEAPON	RANGE	TYPE	S	AP	D	ABILITIES
Master-crafted occulus bolt carbine	24"	Rapid Fire 1	4	0	2	Add 1 to hit rolls for this weapon when targeting a model that is obscured.

ABILITIES	
	And They Shall Know No Fear: You can re-roll failed Nerve tests for this model.
	Transhuman Physiology: Ignore the penalty to this model's hit rolls from one flesh wound it has suffered.
	Knife Fighter: Each unmodified hit roll of 6 made for attacks with this model's close combat weapon scores 2 hits instead of 1.
	Grav-chute: This model never suffers falling damage, and never falls on another model. If it would, instead place this model as close as possible to the point where it would have landed. This can bring it within 1" of an enemy model.
SPECIALISTS	Ferocity, Fortitude, Leadership, Logistics, Melee, Shooting, Stealth, Strategist, Strength
FACTION KEYWORD	ADEPTUS ASTARTES
KEYWORDS	IMPERIUM, COMMANDER, INFANTRY, PHOBOS, PRIMARIS, GRAV-CHUTE, LIEUTENANT

TACTICAL PRECISION

Adeptus Astartes Tactic
Lieutenant in Phobos Armour
Aura Tactic

Use this Tactic at the start of the Shooting phase if your kill team includes a **PHOBOS LIEUTENANT**. That model gains the following aura ability until the end of the battle round:

As long as this model is not shaken, you can re-roll wound rolls of 1 for friendly models within 6" of this model.

1 COMMAND POINT

ADEPTUS ASTARTES

MODEL	POINTS PER MODEL
Lieutenant in Phobos Armour (Level 1)	51
Lieutenant in Phobos Armour (Level 2)	66
Lieutenant in Phobos Armour (Level 3)	81
Lieutenant in Phobos Armour (Level 4)	106

WARGEAR	POINTS PER ITEM
Bolt pistol	0
Close combat weapon	0
Frag grenades	0
Krak grenades	0
Master-crafted occulus bolt carbine	0

LIBRARIAN IN PHOBOS ARMOR

NAME	M	WS	BS	S	T	W	A	Ld	Sv	Max
Librarian in Phobos Armour	6"	3+	3+	4	4	5	4	9	3+	1

This model is armed with a force sword, bolt pistol, frag grenades and krak grenades.

WEAPON	RANGE	TYPE	S	AP	D	ABILITIES
Force sword	Melee	Melee	User	-3	D3	-

ABILITIES	**And They Shall Know No Fear:** You can re-roll failed Nerve tests for this model.
	Transhuman Physiology: Ignore the penalty to this model's hit rolls from one flesh wound it has suffered.
	Camo Cloak: When an opponent makes a hit roll for a shooting attack that targets this model, and this model is obscured, that hit roll suffers an additional -1 modifier.
	Concealed Position: When you set this model up during deployment, it can be set up anywhere on the battlefield that is more than 9" from any enemy deployment zone.
	Psychic Hood: You can add 1 to Deny the Witch tests you take for this model against enemy **PSYKERS** within 12".
PSYKER	This model can attempt to manifest two psychic powers and deny one psychic power in each Psychic phase. It knows the *Psybolt* psychic power as well as two psychic powers generated from the Obscuration discipline (see below).
SPECIALISTS	**Fortitude, Melee, Psyker, Stealth, Strength**
FACTION KEYWORD	**ADEPTUS ASTARTES**
KEYWORDS	**IMPERIUM, COMMANDER, INFANTRY, PHOBOS, PRIMARIS, PSYKER, LIBRARIAN**

OBSCURATION DISCIPLINE

To generate psychic powers from the Obscuration discipline, you can either roll a D3 to generate them randomly (re-roll any duplicate results), or you can select those you wish the psyker to have. Do so before each battle.

D3	RESULT

1 SHROUDING

The psyker uses his mastery of the warp to fog the minds of his enemies, clouding their senses so that his allies appear as nothing more than indistinct shadows.

Shrouding has a warp charge value of 6. If manifested, select a friendly **ADEPTUS ASTARTES PHOBOS** model within 8" of the psyker. Until the start of the next Psychic phase, enemy models can only shoot this model if it is the closest target that is visible to them.

2 HALLUCINATION

The psyker conjures images out of his foes' own memories – from past allies seemingly returned from the dead, to apparitions wrought from their darkest nightmares. Paranoia, confusion and panic reign under such a psychic assault.

Hallucination has a warp charge value of 7. If manifested, select an enemy model within 12" of and visible to the psyker. Until the start of the next Psychic phase, subtract 1 from that model's Leadership characteristic and from hit rolls made for that model.

3 MIND RAID

The psyker raids the thoughts of a foe for tactical information, simultaneously inflicting severe cerebral trauma on his victim.

Mind Raid has a warp charge value of 6. If manifested, select an enemy model within 18" of and visible to the psyker. That model suffers a mortal wound. If your kill team is Battle-forged, and the model you chose was a Leader or a **COMMANDER**, you gain 1 Command Point.

ADEPTUS ASTARTES	
MODEL	**POINTS PER MODEL**
Librarian in Phobos Armour (Level 1)	91
Librarian in Phobos Armour (Level 2)	111
Librarian in Phobos Armour (Level 3)	131
Librarian in Phobos Armour (Level 4)	156
WARGEAR	**POINTS PER ITEM**
Bolt pistol	0
Force sword	0
Frag grenades	0
Krak grenades	0

LIBRARIAN IN TERMINATOR ARMOUR

NAME	M	WS	BS	S	T	W	A	Ld	Sv	Max
Librarian in Terminator Armour	5"	3+	3+	4	4	5	3	9	2+	1

This model is armed with a force stave.

WEAPON	RANGE	TYPE	S	AP	D	ABILITIES
Force axe	Melee	Melee	+1	-2	D3	-
Force stave	Melee	Melee	+2	-1	D3	-
Force sword	Melee	Melee	User	-3	D3	-

WARGEAR OPTIONS	• This model may take a combi-flamer, combi-melta, combi-plasma or storm bolter. • This model may replace its force stave with a force axe or force sword.
ABILITIES	**And They Shall Know No Fear:** You can re-roll failed Nerve tests for this model. **Crux Terminatus:** This model has a 5+ invulnerable save. **Psychic Hood:** You can add 1 to Deny the Witch tests you take for this model against enemy **Psykers** within 12". **Transhuman Physiology:** Ignore the penalty to this model's hit rolls from one flesh wound it has suffered.
PSYKER	This model can attempt to manifest two psychic powers and deny one psychic power in each Psychic phase. It knows the *Psybolt* psychic power as well as two psychic powers generated from the Librarius discipline (see *Kill Team: Commanders*).
SPECIALISTS	**Fortitude, Melee, Psyker, Shooting, Strength**
FACTION KEYWORD	**ADEPTUS ASTARTES**
KEYWORDS	**IMPERIUM, COMMANDER, INFANTRY, TERMINATOR, PSYKER, LIBRARIAN**

ADEPTUS ASTARTES

MODEL	POINTS PER MODEL
Librarian in Terminator Armour (Level 1)	88
Librarian in Terminator Armour (Level 2)	108
Librarian in Terminator Armour (Level 3)	128
Librarian in Terminator Armour (Level 4)	153

WARGEAR	POINTS PER ITEM
Combi-flamer	6
Combi-melta	12
Combi-plasma	9
Force axe	2
Force stave	0
Force sword	0
Storm bolter	4

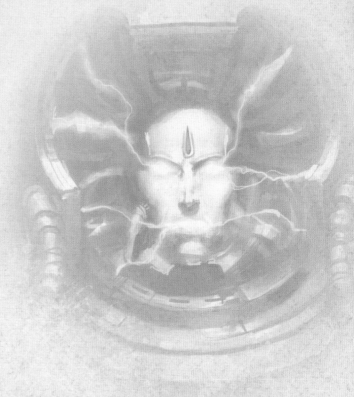

CHAPLAIN IN TERMINATOR ARMOUR

NAME	M	WS	BS	S	T	W	A	Ld	Sv	Max
Chaplain in Terminator Armour	5"	2+	3+	4	4	5	3	9	2+	1

This model is armed with a crozius arcanum and storm bolter.

WEAPON	RANGE	TYPE	S	AP	D	ABILITIES
Crozius arcanum	Melee	Melee	+1	-1	2	-

WARGEAR OPTIONS	• This model may replace its storm bolter with a combi-flamer, combi-melta or combi-plasma.
ABILITIES	**And They Shall Know No Fear:** You can re-roll failed Nerve tests for this model. **Rosarius:** This model has a 4+ invulnerable save. **Transhuman Physiology:** Ignore the penalty to this model's hit rolls from one flesh wound it has suffered.
SPECIALISTS	Ferocity, Fortitude, Leadership, Melee, Shooting, Strength
FACTION KEYWORD	ADEPTUS ASTARTES
KEYWORDS	IMPERIUM, COMMANDER, INFANTRY, TERMINATOR, CHAPLAIN

LITANIES OF HATE

Adeptus Astartes/Deathwatch Tactic
Chaplain in Terminator Armour
Aura Tactic

Use this Tactic at the start of the Fight phase if your kill team includes a TERMINATOR CHAPLAIN. That model gains the following aura ability until the end of the battle round:

As long as this model is not shaken, you can re-roll failed hit rolls in the Fight phase for friendly models within 6" of this model.

1 COMMAND POINT

SPIRITUAL LEADER

Adeptus Astartes/Deathwatch Tactic
Chaplain in Terminator Armour
Aura Tactic

Use this Tactic at the start of the Movement phase if your kill team includes a TERMINATOR CHAPLAIN. That model gains the following aura ability until the end of the battle round:

As long as this model is not shaken, friendly models within 6" of this model can use this model's Leadership characteristic instead of their own.

1 COMMAND POINT

ADEPTUS ASTARTES

MODEL	POINTS PER MODEL
Chaplain in Terminator Armour (Level 1)	74
Chaplain in Terminator Armour (Level 2)	94
Chaplain in Terminator Armour (Level 3)	114
Chaplain in Terminator Armour (Level 4)	139

WARGEAR	POINTS PER ITEM
Combi-flamer	2
Combi-melta	8
Combi-plasma	5
Crozius arcanum	0
Storm bolter	0

CAPTAIN IN TERMINATOR ARMOUR

NAME	M	WS	BS	S	T	W	A	Ld	Sv	Max
Captain in Terminator Armour	5"	2+	2+	4	4	6	4	9	2+	1

This model is armed with a power sword and storm bolter.

WEAPON	RANGE	TYPE	S	AP	D	ABILITIES
Wrist-mounted grenade launcher	12"	Assault D3	4	-1	1	-

WARGEAR OPTIONS	
	• This model may replace its storm bolter with a combi-flamer, combi-melta, combi-plasma or one item from the *Terminator Weapons* list (pg 42).
	• This model may replace its power sword with a chainfist or one item from the *Terminator Weapons* list (pg 42).
	• A Captain in Terminator Armour with a power fist can also be armed with a wrist-mounted grenade launcher.

ABILITIES	
	And They Shall Know No Fear: You can re-roll failed Nerve tests for this model.
	Transhuman Physiology: Ignore the penalty to this model's hit rolls from one flesh wound it has suffered.
	Iron Halo or Storm Shield: This model has a 4+ invulnerable save. If it is armed with a storm shield, it instead has a 3+ invulnerable save.

SPECIALISTS	**Ferocity**, **Fortitude**, **Leadership**, **Logistics**, **Melee**, **Shooting**, **Strategist**, **Strength**
FACTION KEYWORD	ADEPTUS ASTARTES
KEYWORDS	IMPERIUM, COMMANDER, INFANTRY, TERMINATOR, CAPTAIN

RITES OF BATTLE

Adeptus Astartes/Deathwatch Tactic
Captain in Terminator Armour
Aura Tactic

Use this Tactic at the start of the Shooting phase if your kill team includes a **TERMINATOR CAPTAIN**. That model gains the following aura ability until the end of the battle round:

As long as this model is not shaken, you can re-roll hit rolls of 1 for friendly models within 6" of this model.

1 COMMAND POINT

ADEPTUS ASTARTES

MODEL	POINTS PER MODEL
Captain in Terminator Armour (Level 1)	80
Captain in Terminator Armour (Level 2)	100
Captain in Terminator Armour (Level 3)	120
Captain in Terminator Armour (Level 4)	145

WARGEAR	POINTS PER ITEM
Chainfist	13
Combi-flamer	2
Combi-melta	8
Combi-plasma	5
Lightning claw (single/pair)	4/8
Power axe	2
Power fist	12
Power maul	0
Power sword	0
Relic blade	14
Storm bolter	0
Storm shield	15
Thunder hammer	18
Wrist-mounted grenade launcher	2

INFILTRATOR

NAME	M	WS	BS	S	T	W	A	Ld	Sv	Max
Infiltrator	6"	3+	3+	4	4	2	2	7	3+	-
Infiltrator Helix Adept	6"	3+	3+	4	4	2	2	7	3+	1
Infiltrator Sergeant	6"	3+	3+	4	4	2	3	8	3+	1

This model is armed with a marksman bolt carbine, bolt pistol, frag grenades and krak grenades.
One Infiltrator in your kill team can be an Infiltrator Helix Adept, and one Infiltrator in your kill team can be an Infiltrator Sergeant.

ABILITIES	**And They Shall Know No Fear:** You can re-roll failed Nerve tests for this model.	**Concealed Position:** When you set this model up during deployment, it can be set up anywhere on the battlefield that is more than 9" from any enemy deployment zone.
	Transhuman Physiology: Ignore the penalty to this model's hit rolls from one flesh wound it has suffered.	**Omni-scrambler:** Enemy models that are set up on the battlefield from Reserve cannot be set up within 7" of this model.

SPECIALISTS	**Leader** (Sergeant only), **Medic** (Helix Adept only), **Comms**, **Demolitions**, **Scout**, **Stealth**, **Veteran**
FACTION KEYWORD	**ADEPTUS ASTARTES**
KEYWORDS	**IMPERIUM, INFANTRY, PHOBOS, PRIMARIS, INFILTRATOR**

SUPPRESSOR

NAME	M	WS	BS	S	T	W	A	Ld	Sv	Max
Suppressor	12"	3+	3+	4	4	2	2	7	3+	-
Suppressor Sergeant	12"	3+	3+	4	4	2	3	8	3+	1

This model is armed with an accelerator autocannon, bolt pistol, frag grenades and krak grenades.
One Suppressor in your kill team can be a Suppressor Sergeant.

ABILITIES	**And They Shall Know No Fear:** You can re-roll failed Nerve tests for this model.	**Grav-chute:** This model never suffers falling damage, and never falls on another model. If it would, instead place this model as close as possible to the point where it would have landed. This can bring it within 1" of an enemy model.
	Transhuman Physiology: Ignore the penalty to this model's hit rolls from one flesh wound it has suffered.	

SPECIALISTS	**Leader** (Sergeant only), **Demolitions**, **Scout**, **Sniper**, **Stealth**, **Veteran**
FACTION KEYWORD	**ADEPTUS ASTARTES**
KEYWORDS	**IMPERIUM, INFANTRY, FLY, PHOBOS, PRIMARIS, GRAV-CHUTE, SUPPRESSOR**

ELIMINATOR

NAME	M	WS	BS	S	T	W	A	Ld	Sv	Max
Eliminator	6"	3+	3+	4	4	2	2	7	3+	-
Eliminator Sergeant	6"	3+	3+	4	4	2	3	8	3+	1

This model is armed with a bolt sniper rifle, bolt pistol, frag grenades and krak grenades.
One Eliminator in your kill team can be an Eliminator Sergeant.

ABILITIES	**And They Shall Know No Fear:** You can re-roll failed Nerve tests for this model. **Transhuman Physiology:** Ignore the penalty to this model's hit rolls from one flesh wound it has suffered.	**Camo Cloak:** When an opponent makes a hit roll for a shooting attack that targets this model, and this model is obscured, that hit roll suffers an additional -1 modifier. **Concealed Position:** When you set this model up during deployment, it can be set up anywhere on the battlefield that is more than 9" from any enemy deployment zone.
SPECIALISTS	**Leader** (Sergeant only), **Comms**, **Scout**, **Sniper**, **Stealth**, **Veteran**	
FACTION KEYWORD	**Adeptus Astartes**	
KEYWORDS	**Imperium, Infantry, Phobos, Primaris, Eliminator**	

TERMINATOR

NAME	M	WS	BS	S	T	W	A	Ld	Sv	Max
Terminator	5"	3+	3+	4	4	2	2	8	2+	-
Terminator Gunner	5"	3+	3+	4	4	2	2	8	2+	2
Terminator Sergeant	5"	3+	3+	4	4	2	3	9	2+	1

This model is armed with a power fist and storm bolter.
Up to two Terminators in your kill team can be Terminator Gunners, and one Terminator in your kill team can be a Terminator Sergeant.
A Terminator Sergeant is armed with a power sword and storm bolter.

WARGEAR OPTIONS	• A Terminator or Terminator Gunner may replace their power fist with a chainfist. • A Terminator Gunner may replace their storm bolter with an assault cannon, heavy flamer or cyclone missile launcher and a storm bolter. • A Terminator or Terminator Sergeant may replace their power fist (or power sword) and storm bolter with a pair of lightning claws or a thunder hammer and storm shield. • A **Space Wolves** Terminator, Terminator Gunner or Terminator Sergeant may replace their power fist or power sword with a lightning claw, power axe, power maul, power sword, storm shield or thunder hammer. • A **Space Wolves** Terminator, Terminator Gunner or Terminator Sergeant may replace their storm bolter with a combi-flamer, combi-melta, combi-plasma or one item from the *Terminator Weapons* list (pg 42). • A **Dark Angels** Terminator Gunner may replace their storm bolter with a plasma cannon.	
ABILITIES	**And They Shall Know No Fear:** You can re-roll failed Nerve tests for this model. **Transhuman Physiology:** Ignore the penalty to this model's hit rolls from one flesh wound it has suffered.	**Crux Terminatus or Storm Shield:** This model has a 5+ invulnerable save. If it is armed with a storm shield, it instead has a 3+ invulnerable save.
SPECIALISTS	**Leader** (Sergeant only), **Heavy** (Gunner only), **Combat**, **Comms**, **Demolitions**, **Veteran**, **Zealot**	
FACTION KEYWORD	**Adeptus Astartes**	
KEYWORDS	**Imperium, Infantry, Terminator**	

VETERAN

NAME	M	WS	BS	S	T	W	A	Ld	Sv	Max
Sternguard Veteran	6"	3+	3+	4	4	1	2	8	3+	-
Vanguard Veteran	6"	3+	3+	4	4	1	2	8	3+	-
Company Veteran	6"	3+	3+	4	4	1	2	8	3+	4
Sternguard Gunner	6"	3+	3+	4	4	1	2	8	3+	2
Sternguard Sergeant	6"	3+	3+	4	4	1	3	9	3+	1
Vanguard Sergeant	6"	3+	3+	4	4	1	3	9	3+	1
Veteran Sergeant	6"	3+	3+	4	4	1	3	9	3+	1

A Veteran is a Sternguard Veteran, a Vanguard Veteran or a Company Veteran. A Sternguard Veteran is armed with a special issue boltgun, bolt pistol, frag grenades and krak grenades. A Vanguard Veteran or Company Veteran is instead armed with a chainsword, bolt pistol, frag grenades and krak grenades.

Up to two Sternguard Veterans in your kill team can be Sternguard Gunners, and one Sternguard Veteran in your kill team can be a Sternguard Sergeant. One Vanguard Veteran in your kill team can be a Vanguard Sergeant. One Company Veteran in your kill team can be a Veteran Sergeant.

SPACE WOLVES and **DARK ANGELS** models cannot be Sternguard Veterans, Sternguard Gunners, Sternguard Sergeants, Vanguard Veterans or Vanguard Sergeants, and the Max characteristic for **SPACE WOLVES** Company Veterans is '-' (rather than 4).

WARGEAR OPTIONS	• A Sternguard Veteran may exchange their special issue boltgun for one item from the *Combi-weapons* list (pg 42).
	• A Sternguard Gunner may exchange their special issue boltgun for one item from the *Combi-weapons* or *Heavy Weapons* lists (pg 42).
	• A Sternguard Sergeant may be equipped with an auspex.
	• A Sternguard Sergeant or Veteran Sergeant may exchange their special issue boltgun (or boltgun) and bolt pistol for up to two items from the *Pistols* and/or *Melee Weapons* lists, and if they do so they may also take a special issue boltgun (or boltgun, for a Veteran Sergeant) or up to one item from the *Combi-weapons* list (pg 42).
	• A Sternguard Sergeant, Company Veteran or Veteran Sergeant may exchange their bolt pistol for one item from the *Pistols* or *Melee Weapons* lists (pg 42).
	• A Company Veteran may exchange their chainsword for a boltgun or one item from the *Combi-weapons*, *Special Weapons*, *Pistols* or *Melee Weapons* lists (pg 42).
	• A Vanguard Veteran or Vanguard Sergeant may exchange their bolt pistol and chainsword for two items from the *Pistols* and/or *Melee Weapons* lists (pg 42).
	• A Vanguard Veteran or Vanguard Sergeant may be equipped with a jump pack. If they are, their Move characteristic is increased to 12" and they gain the **JUMP PACK** and **FLY** keywords.
	• One Vanguard Veteran or Vanguard Sergeant in your kill team may be armed with melta bombs.
	• One **DARK ANGELS** Company Veteran in your kill team may exchange their boltgun with one weapon from the *Heavy Weapons* list.
	• A **DARK ANGELS** Company Veteran or **DARK ANGELS** Veteran Sergeant may be armed with a combat shield. A model armed with a combat shield has a 5+ invulnerable save.
	• A **SPACE WOLVES** Company Veteran or **SPACE WOLVES** Veteran Sergeant may be equipped with a jump pack. If they are, their Move characteristic is increased to 12" and they gain the **JUMP PACK** and **FLY** keywords.

ABILITIES	**And They Shall Know No Fear:** You can re-roll failed Nerve tests for this model.	**Auspex:** At the start of the Shooting phase, you can choose another **ADEPTUS ASTARTES** model within 3" of a friendly model equipped with an auspex that is not shaken. That model does not suffer penalties to their hit or Injury rolls due to their target being obscured.
	Transhuman Physiology: Ignore the penalty to this model's hit rolls from one flesh wound it has suffered.	
	Storm Shield: A model armed with a storm shield has a 3+ invulnerable save.	

SPECIALISTS	**Leader** (Sergeant only), **Heavy** (Gunner only), **Combat**, **Comms**, **Demolitions**, **Sniper**, **Veteran**, **Zealot**
FACTION KEYWORD	**ADEPTUS ASTARTES**
KEYWORDS	**IMPERIUM, INFANTRY, STERNGUARD VETERAN/VANGUARD VETERAN/COMPANY VETERAN**

RANGED WEAPONS

WEAPON	RANGE	TYPE	S	AP	D	ABILITIES
Accelerator autocannon	48"	Heavy 2	7	-2	2	If this weapon inflicts any damage on an enemy model, until the end of the battle round that model and enemy models within 2" of that model cannot make shooting attacks.
Assault cannon	24"	Heavy 6	6	-1	1	-
Bolt sniper rifle						A model firing a bolt sniper rifle does not suffer the penalty to hit rolls for the target being at long range. In addition, when attacking with this weapon, choose one of the profiles below.
- Executioner round	36"	Heavy 1	4	-2	D3	If you make a wound roll of 6+ for this weapon, it inflicts a mortal wound in addition to its normal damage.
- Mortis round	36"	Heavy 1	4	-1	1	Add 2 to hit rolls made for this weapon. In addition, this weapon can target models that are not visible to the bearer. If the target is not visible to the bearer, a 6 is required for a successful hit roll, irrespective of the firing model's Ballistic Skill or any modifiers.
- Hyperfrag round	36"	Heavy D3	4	0	1	-
Cyclone missile launcher						When attacking with this weapon, choose one of the profiles below.
- Frag missile	36"	Heavy 2D3	4	0	1	-
- Krak missile	36"	Heavy 2	8	-2	D6	-
Grav-cannon and grav-amp	24"	Heavy 4	5	-3	1	If the target has a Save characteristic of 3+ or better, this weapon has a Damage of D3.
Hand flamer	6"	Pistol D3	3	0	1	This weapon automatically hits its target.
Heavy flamer	8"	Heavy D6	5	-1	1	This weapon automatically hits its target.
Inferno pistol	6"	Pistol 1	8	-4	D6	If the target is within half range of this weapon, roll two dice when inflicting damage with it and discard the lowest result.
Lascannon	48"	Heavy 1	9	-3	D6	-
Marksman bolt carbine	24"	Rapid Fire 1	4	0	1	Each unmodified hit roll of 6 made for this weapon's attacks automatically results in a wound (do not make a wound roll for that attack).
Melta bomb	4"	Grenade 1	8	-4	D6	-
Meltagun	12"	Assault 1	8	-4	D6	If the target is within half range of this weapon, roll two dice when inflicting damage with it and discard the lowest result.
Multi-melta	24"	Heavy 1	8	-4	D6	If the target is within half range of this weapon, roll two dice when inflicting damage with it and discard the lowest result.
Plasma cannon						When attacking with this weapon, choose one of the profiles below.
- Standard	36"	Heavy D3	7	-3	1	-
- Supercharge	36"	Heavy D3	8	-3	2	On an unmodified hit roll of 1, the bearer is taken out of action after all of this weapon's shots have been resolved.
Special issue boltgun	30"	Rapid Fire 1	4	-2	1	-
Storm bolter	24"	Rapid Fire 2	4	0	1	-

MELEE WEAPONS

WEAPON	RANGE	TYPE	S	AP	D	ABILITIES
Chainfist	Melee	Melee	x2	-4	2	When attacking with this weapon, you must subtract 1 from the hit roll.
Close combat weapon	Melee	Melee	User	0	1	-
Lightning claw	Melee	Melee	User	-2	1	You can re-roll failed wound rolls for this weapon. If a model is armed with two lightning claws, each time it fights it can make 1 additional attack with them.
Power axe	Melee	Melee	+1	-2	1	-
Power maul	Melee	Melee	+2	-1	1	-
Relic blade	Melee	Melee	+2	-3	D3	-
Thunder hammer	Melee	Melee	x2	-3	3	When attacking with this weapon, you must subtract 1 from the hit roll.

WARGEAR LISTS

PISTOLS

Bolt pistol

Grav-pistol (cannot be taken by **Space Wolves**)

Hand flamer (**Blood Angels** only)

Inferno pistol (**Blood Angels** only)

Plasma pistol

MELEE WEAPONS

Chainsword

Lightning claw

Power axe

Power fist

Power maul (**Dark Angels** only)

Power sword

Relic blade (Vanguard Sergeant only)

Storm shield (cannot be taken by Sternguard Sergeants)

Thunder hammer (cannot be taken by Sternguard Sergeants)

COMBI-WEAPONS

Combi-flamer

Combi-grav (cannot be taken by **Space Wolves**)

Combi-melta

Combi-plasma

Storm bolter

SPECIAL WEAPONS

Flamer

Grav-gun

Meltagun

Plasma gun

HEAVY WEAPONS

Grav-cannon and grav-amp

Heavy bolter

Heavy flamer (**Sternguard** only)

Lascannon

Missile launcher

Multi-melta

Plasma cannon

TERMINATOR WEAPONS

Chainfist (**Space Wolves** only)

Lightning claw

Power axe (**Space Wolves** only)

Power fist

Power maul (**Space Wolves** only)

Power sword (**Space Wolves** only)

Relic blade (cannot be taken by **Space Wolves** or a model with a chainfist)

Storm shield

Thunder hammer

KILL TEAM

MODEL	POINTS PER MODEL (Does not include wargear)
Eliminator	18
- Eliminator Sergeant	19
Infiltrator	17
- Infiltrator Helix Adept	18
- Infiltrator Sergeant	18
Veteran	-
- Sternguard Veteran	13
- Vanguard Veteran	13
- Company Veteran	13
- Sternguard Gunner	14
- Sternguard Sergeant	14
- Vanguard Sergeant	14
- Veteran Sergeant	14
Suppressor	29
- Suppressor Sergeant	30
Terminator	25
- Terminator Gunner	26
- Terminator Sergeant	27

RANGED WEAPONS

WEAPON	POINTS PER WEAPON
Accelerator autocannon	0
Assault cannon	5
Bolt pistol	0
Bolt sniper rifle	0
Boltgun	0
Combi-flamer	5
Combi-grav	4
Combi-melta	9
Combi-plasma	7
Cyclone missile launcher	6
Flamer	3
Frag grenades	0
Grav-cannon and grav-amp	5
Grav-gun	2
Grav-pistol	1
Hand flamer	0
Heavy bolter	3
Heavy flamer	5
Inferno pistol	8
Krak grenades	0
Lascannon	13
Marksman bolt carbine	0
Melta bombs	5
Meltagun	7
Missile launcher	10
Multi-melta	10
Plasma cannon	12
Plasma gun	5
Plasma pistol	2
Special issue boltgun	1
Storm bolter	2

MELEE WEAPONS	
WEAPON	POINTS PER WEAPON
Chainfist	6
Chainsword	0
Lightning claw (single/pair)	1/3
Power axe	2
Power fist	4
Power maul	1
Power sword	1
Relic blade	3
Thunder hammer	8

OTHER WARGEAR	
WARGEAR	POINTS PER ITEM
Auspex	1
Combat shield	5
Jump pack	6
Storm shield	5

DEATHWATCH KILL TEAMS

Deathwatch models in your kill team use the Special Issue Ammunition ability below. If every model in your kill team has the DEATHWATCH Faction keyword, models in your kill team gain the Mission Tactics ability, below, and you can use Deathwatch Tactics.

Mission Tactics: At the beginning of the first battle round, choose a datasheet to be your kill team's priority target (e.g. Tyranid Warrior). You can re-roll wound rolls of 1 for attacks made by models in your kill team that target a model from the datasheet that is your kill team's priority target (so if you chose Tyranid Warrior, this ability would apply to attacks that targeted Tyranid Warriors and Tyranid Warrior Gunners).

TACTICAL PRIORITY

Deathwatch Tactic

Use this Tactic at the start of any battle round after the first. When you do, choose a datasheet. That datasheet is now your kill team's priority target as described in Mission Tactics (above), rather than the datasheet you chose previously.

1 COMMAND POINT

Special Issue Ammunition: When this model fires an auto bolt rifle, bolt carbine, bolt pistol, bolt rifle, boltgun, combi-flamer (boltgun profile only), combi-melta (boltgun profile only), combi-plasma (boltgun profile only), heavy bolt pistol, stalker bolt rifle, stalker pattern boltgun or storm bolter, you can choose one kind of ammunition from the table below, and apply the corresponding modifier.

Aquila Kill Team: When you add a Captain in Terminator Armour (pg 37), Chaplain in Terminator Armour (pg 36), Librarian in Terminator Armour (pg 35), Terminator (pg 39) or Veteran (which must be a Vanguard Veteran equipped with a jump pack, pg 40) to your command roster (and create its datacard) you can choose for it to have the DEATHWATCH Faction keyword instead of the ADEPTUS ASTARTES Faction keyword. If you do so, it gains the Special Issue Ammunition ability but you must add the relevant additional point values opposite to the model's total points if it is equipped with any of the ranged weapons opposite.

RANGED WEAPONS (SPECIAL ISSUE AMMUNITION)

WEAPON	POINTS PER WEAPON
Bolt pistol	+2
Combi-flamer	+2
Combi-melta	+2
Combi-plasma	+2
Storm bolter	+4

SPECIAL ISSUE AMMUNITION

AMMUNITION	MODIFIER
Dragonfire bolt	Add 1 to hit rolls for this weapon when targeting a model that is obscured.
Hellfire round	This weapon always wounds on a 2+.
Kraken bolt	Add 3" to the range of this weapon if it is a Pistol – or 6" otherwise – and improve the AP of the attack by 1 (e.g. an AP of 0 becomes -1), to a maximum AP of -2.
Vengeance round	Subtract 3" from the range of this weapon if it is a Pistol – or 6" otherwise – and improve the AP of the attack by 2 (e.g. an AP of 0 becomes -2), to a maximum AP of -3.

GREY KNIGHTS

The Grey Knights are the ultimate Imperial weapon against the malign entities of the warp. A secret Chapter of Adeptus Astartes warriors operating from a hidden stronghold on the moon of Titan, these unsung heroes have prevented the Imperium from succumbing to a Daemon apocalypse time and time again.

Even amongst the ranks of the Adeptus Astartes, the Grey Knights are truly remarkable. Unlike their estranged brothers in the other Space Marine Chapters, the Grey Knights are kept secret from the wider Imperium and hidden from the prying eyes of its many foes. In the first instance, this is because – were the wider peoples of the Imperium to learn the true horror of the enemies that the Grey Knights face – madness and terror would spread like wildfire. Yet the very secrecy of this elite order is also a weapon unto itself, for the first the Grey Knights' enemies know of these silver-clad killers is when they appear as if from nowhere with bolters blazing and blades flashing.

Beyond the normal range of genetic enhancements and advanced weaponry possessed by all Space Marines, the Grey Knights are rendered even more deadly by the fact that every single one of them is a potent psyker. So formidable are the Grey Knights' powers, and so impregnable their mental defences, that they can see off even the most terrible psychic assaults and banish warp-manifestations through their phenomenal willpower alone.

Of course, every Grey Knight is also an exceptionally skilled warrior, and their most veteran heroes and leaders are amongst the Imperium's greatest defenders. Squads of Grey Knights Terminators stride into battle clad in nigh-impregnable suits of blessed Terminator armour. Able to shrug off direct hits from tank-busting weaponry and stride heedless through screaming artillery bombardments, Grey Knights Terminators advance with the inexorable determination of death itself. Their storm bolters, psycannons and incinerators sweep away rank upon rank of enemies, before their crackling Nemesis force weapons make short work at close-quarters of those few who survive.

Even more powerful are the Paladins of the Grey Knights, those warriors who have completed great quests in order to prove themselves paragons of combat and mental fortitude. Be it seething tides of Daemons or the irrevocably corrupt and seemingly unstoppable warriors of the Heretic Astartes, the Paladins scythe through them with sweeping blows from their sanctified blades and devastating blasts of psychic force.

The grim-faced leaders of the 666th Chapter are the greatest heroes of all. Grey Knights Librarians and Brother-Captains are unstoppable and frighteningly determined warriors. Possessed of towering psychic might, they wield weapons whose worth can be measured in worlds and wear gleaming Terminator plate inscribed with complex canticles of warding. No danger is too terrible, no enemy too gruesome or sanity-blasting for them to lay low. Even a single such combatant is the equal of countless lesser enemies, but when they lead a kill team of elite Grey Knights into battle, they are truly unstoppable.

GREY KNIGHTS KILL TEAMS

If every model in your kill team has the GREY KNIGHTS Faction keyword, models in your kill team gain the Brotherhood of Psykers ability below, and you can use Grey Knights Tactics.

Brotherhood of Psykers: When it is your turn to choose a PSYKER from your kill team to attempt to manifest psychic powers in this phase, you can choose up to two models from your kill team to do so. Resolve all of one model's attempts before choosing the next model. In addition, you can add 1 to Psychic tests and Deny the Witch tests for models in your kill team.

TELEPORT STRIKE

Grey Knights Tactic

Use this Tactic at the end of the Movement phase. Choose up to three TERMINATOR models from your kill team that were set up in Reserve and set them up anywhere on the battlefield that is more than 5" away from any enemy models.

1 COMMAND POINT

LIBRARIAN

NAME	M	WS	BS	S	T	W	A	Ld	Sv	Max
Librarian	5"	2+	2+	4	4	5	3	9	2+	1

This model is armed with a Nemesis warding stave, frag grenades, krak grenades and psyk-out grenades.

WARGEAR OPTIONS	• This model may take a combi-flamer, combi-melta, combi plasma or storm bolter. • This model may replace its Nemesis warding stave with a Nemesis Daemon hammer, Nemesis force halberd, Nemesis force sword or two Nemesis falchions.
ABILITIES	**And They Shall Know No Fear, Daemon Hunters, Rites of Banishment, Transhuman Physiology** (see opposite), **Crux Terminatus** (pg 48) **Psychic Hood:** You can add 1 to Deny the Witch tests you take for this model against enemy **PSYKERS** within 12".
PSYKER	This model can attempt to manifest two psychic powers and deny two psychic powers in each Psychic phase. It knows the *Psybolt* psychic power as well as two psychic powers generated from the Sanctic discipline (see below).
SPECIALISTS	**Fortitude, Melee, Psyker, Shooting, Strength**
FACTION KEYWORD	**GREY KNIGHTS**
KEYWORDS	**IMPERIUM, ADEPTUS ASTARTES, COMMANDER, INFANTRY, TERMINATOR, PSYKER, LIBRARIAN**

SANCTIC DISCIPLINE

To generate psychic powers from the Sanctic discipline, you can either roll a D3 to generate them randomly (re-roll any duplicate results), or you can select those you wish the psyker to have. Do so before each battle.

D3 RESULT

1 GATE OF INFINITY

The psyker punches a corridor through the roiling immaterium, allowing him to cross great distances in the blink of an eye.

Gate of Infinity has a warp charge value of 6. If manifested, pick a friendly model within 8" of the psyker. Remove that model from the battlefield and immediately set it up anywhere on the battlefield that is more than 5" from any enemy models. The model is not considered to have charged or been charged in the next Fight phase.

2 HAMMERHAND

Focusing the raging power of his mind, the psyker augments the strength of his comrades to the point where they can crush flesh and bone with a single blow.

Hammerhand has a warp charge value of 5. If manifested, pick a friendly model within 12" of the psyker. Add 1 to wound rolls you make for that model's Melee weapons until the start of the next Psychic phase.

3 SANCTUARY

Chanting words of warding, the psyker creates a zone of light around him that can both protect him from harm and repel daemonic creatures.

Sanctuary has a warp charge value of 6. If manifested, pick a GREY KNIGHTS model within 8" of the psyker. That model gains a 5+ invulnerable save until the start of the next Psychic phase. If the model already has an invulnerable save, improve that save by 1 (to a maximum of 3+) until the start of the next Psychic phase instead.

GREY KNIGHTS	
MODEL	**POINTS PER MODEL**
Librarian (Level 1)	96
Librarian (Level 2)	116
Librarian (Level 3)	136
Librarian (Level 4)	161
WARGEAR	**POINTS PER ITEM**
Combi-flamer	12
Combi-melta	14
Combi-plasma	12
Frag grenades	0
Krak grenades	0
Nemesis Daemon hammer	8
Nemesis falchion	0
Nemesis force halberd	0
Nemesis force sword	0
Nemesis warding stave	0
Psyk-out grenades	0
Storm bolter	4

BROTHER-CAPTAIN

NAME	M	WS	BS	S	T	W	A	Ld	Sv	Max
Brother-Captain	5"	2+	2+	4	4	6	4	9	2+	1

This model is armed with a Nemesis force halberd, storm bolter, frag grenades, krak grenades and psyk-out grenades.

WARGEAR OPTIONS	• This model may replace its Nemesis force halberd with a Nemesis Daemon hammer, a Nemesis force sword, a Nemesis warding stave or two Nemesis falchions. • This model may replace its storm bolter with an incinerator, psilencer or psycannon.
ABILITIES	**And They Shall Know No Fear:** You can re-roll failed Nerve tests for this model. **Transhuman Physiology:** Ignore the penalty to this model's hit rolls from one flesh wound it has suffered. **Iron Halo:** This model has a 4+ invulnerable save. **Daemon Hunters:** If this model attacks any **DAEMONS** in the Fight phase, you can re-roll failed wound rolls for those attacks. **Rites of Banishment:** When this model manifests the *Psybolt* psychic power it has a range of 12". If *Psybolt* is successfully manifested, and the target model is a **DAEMON**, the target suffers D3 mortal wounds, even if the result of the Psychic test was not 11+.
PSYKER	This model can attempt to manifest one psychic power and deny one psychic power in each Psychic phase. It knows the *Psybolt* psychic power as well as the *Hammerhand* psychic power (see opposite).
SPECIALISTS	**Ferocity, Fortitude, Leadership, Logistics, Melee, Psyker, Shooting, Strategist, Strength**
FACTION KEYWORD	**GREY KNIGHTS**
KEYWORDS	**IMPERIUM, ADEPTUS ASTARTES, COMMANDER, INFANTRY, TERMINATOR, BROTHER-CAPTAIN**

PSYCHIC LOCUS

Grey Knights Tactic
Brother-Captain Aura Tactic

Use this Tactic at the start of the Psychic phase if your kill team includes a **BROTHER-CAPTAIN**. That model gains the following aura ability until the end of the battle round:

As long as this model is not shaken, the *Psybolt* psychic power affects the closest enemy model within 36" (rather than 12" or 18") of and visible to the psyker when manifested by friendly models within 6" of this model.

1 COMMAND POINT

GREY KNIGHTS

MODEL	POINTS PER MODEL
Brother-Captain (Level 1)	100
Brother-Captain (Level 2)	120
Brother-Captain (Level 3)	140
Brother-Captain (Level 4)	165

WARGEAR	POINTS PER ITEM
Frag grenades	0
Incinerator	3
Krak grenades	0
Nemesis Daemon hammer	8
Nemesis falchion	0
Nemesis force halberd	0
Nemesis force sword	0
Nemesis warding stave	0
Psilencer	16
Psycannon	7
Psyk-out grenades	0
Storm bolter	0

TERMINATOR

NAME	M	WS	BS	S	T	W	A	Ld	Sv	Max
Terminator	5"	3+	3+	4	4	2	2	7	2+	-
Terminator Gunner	5"	3+	3+	4	4	2	2	7	2+	2
Terminator Justicar	5"	3+	3+	4	4	2	3	8	2+	1

This model is armed with a Nemesis force sword, storm bolter, frag grenades, krak grenades and psyk-out grenades.
Up to two Terminators in your kill team can be Terminator Gunners, and one Terminator in your kill team can be a Terminator Justicar.

WARGEAR OPTIONS	• This model may replace its Nemesis force sword with a Nemesis Daemon hammer, a Nemesis force halberd, a Nemesis warding stave or two Nemesis falchions. • A Terminator Gunner may replace their storm bolter with an incinerator, psilencer or psycannon.
ABILITIES	**And They Shall Know No Fear:** You can re-roll failed Nerve tests for this model. **Transhuman Physiology:** Ignore the penalty to this model's hit rolls from one flesh wound it has suffered. **Crux Terminatus:** This model has a 5+ invulnerable save.	**Daemon Hunters:** If this model attacks any **Daemons** in the Fight phase, you can re-roll failed wound rolls for those attacks. **Rites of Banishment:** When this model manifests the *Psybolt* psychic power it has a range of 12". If *Psybolt* is successfully manifested, and the target model is a **Daemon**, the target suffers D3 mortal wounds, even if the result of the Psychic test was not 11+.
PSYKER	This model can attempt to manifest one psychic power and deny one psychic power in each Psychic phase. It knows the *Psybolt* psychic power.
SPECIALISTS	**Leader** (Justicar only), **Heavy** (Gunner only), **Combat**, **Comms**, **Demolitions**, **Veteran**, **Zealot**
FACTION KEYWORD	**Grey Knights**
KEYWORDS	**Imperium, Adeptus Astartes, Infantry, Psyker, Terminator**

PALADIN

NAME	M	WS	BS	S	T	W	A	Ld	Sv	Max
Paladin	5"	3+	3+	4	4	3	3	8	2+	-
Paladin Gunner	5"	3+	3+	4	4	3	3	8	2+	4
Paragon	5"	3+	3+	4	4	3	3	9	2+	1

This model is armed with a Nemesis force sword, storm bolter, frag grenades, krak grenades and psyk-out grenades.
Up to four Paladins in your kill team can be Paladin Gunners, and one Paladin in your kill team can be a Paragon.

WARGEAR OPTIONS	• This model may replace its Nemesis force sword with a Nemesis Daemon hammer, a Nemesis force halberd, a Nemesis warding stave or two Nemesis falchions. • A Paladin Gunner may replace their storm bolter with an incinerator, psilencer or psycannon.
ABILITIES	**And They Shall Know No Fear:** You can re-roll failed Nerve tests for this model. **Transhuman Physiology:** Ignore the penalty to this model's hit rolls from one flesh wound it has suffered. **Crux Terminatus:** This model has a 5+ invulnerable save.	**Daemon Hunters:** If this model attacks any **Daemons** in the Fight phase, you can re-roll failed wound rolls for those attacks. **Rites of Banishment:** When this model manifests the *Psybolt* psychic power it has a range of 12". If *Psybolt* is successfully manifested, and the target model is a **Daemon**, the target suffers D3 mortal wounds, even if the result of the Psychic test was not 11+.
PSYKER	This model can attempt to manifest one psychic power and deny one psychic power in each Psychic phase. It knows the *Psybolt* psychic power.
SPECIALISTS	**Leader** (Paragon only), **Heavy** (Gunner only), **Combat**, **Comms**, **Demolitions**, **Veteran**, **Zealot**
FACTION KEYWORD	**Grey Knights**
KEYWORDS	**Imperium, Adeptus Astartes, Infantry, Psyker, Terminator, Paladin**

RANGED WEAPONS

WEAPON	RANGE	TYPE	S	AP	D	ABILITIES
Combi-flamer	When attacking with this weapon, choose one or both of the profiles below. If you choose both, subtract 1 from all hit rolls made for this weapon.					
- Boltgun	24"	Rapid Fire 1	4	0	1	-
- Flamer	8"	Assault D6	4	0	1	This weapon automatically hits its target.
Combi-melta	When attacking with this weapon, choose one or both of the profiles below. If you choose both, subtract 1 from all hit rolls made for this weapon.					
- Boltgun	24"	Rapid Fire 1	4	0	1	-
- Meltagun	12"	Assault 1	8	-4	D6	If the target is within half range of this weapon, roll two dice when inflicting damage with it and discard the lowest result.
Combi-plasma	When attacking with this weapon, choose one or both of the profiles below. If you choose both, subtract 1 from all hit rolls made for this weapon.					
- Boltgun	24"	Rapid Fire 1	4	0	1	-
- Plasma gun	24"	Rapid Fire 1	7	-3	1	This weapon can be supercharged by the bearer before firing. If they do so, increase the Strength and Damage of the weapon by 1 this turn. On any unmodified hit rolls of 1 when firing supercharge, the bearer is taken out of action after all of the weapon's shots have been resolved.

KILL TEAM

MODEL	POINTS PER MODEL (Does not include wargear)
Terminator	36
- Terminator Gunner	37
- Terminator Justicar	39
Paladin	47
- Paladin Gunner	48
- Paragon	50

RANGED WEAPONS

WEAPON	POINTS PER WEAPON
Frag grenades	0
Incinerator	1
Krak grenades	0
Psilencer	8
Psycannon	4
Psyk-out grenades	0
Storm bolter	0

MELEE WEAPONS

WEAPON	POINTS PER WEAPON
Nemesis Daemon hammer	4
Nemesis falchion	1
Nemesis force halberd	1
Nemesis force sword	0
Nemesis warding stave	3

ADEPTUS MECHANICUS

The Tech-Priests of the Adeptus Mechanicus are masters of the arcane arts of technology. They fight bloody wars to acquire even the smallest fragments of archeotech, and will gladly throw away the lives of their machine-congregations in order to protect their covetously hoarded lore.

The Adeptus Mechanicus are worshippers of the Omnissiah, the Machine God of Mars. It is through their ancient secrets and esoteric rituals that Humanity is furnished with the weapons and machines to continue its war for survival. Without the immense wealth of technological knowledge possessed by the Adeptus Mechanicus, the Emperor's realm would soon collapse into anarchy and barbarism.

Yet the priests of the Martian Cult are far from altruistic saviours. They are grasping and acquisitive, jealous, ruthless and utterly without mercy. They know well the stranglehold they have on the rest of the Imperium, and are quick to exploit it in order to further their own agendas. Almost inevitably, these involve the search for and seizure of artefacts that might lead to further technological revelations, and the Tech-Priests do not baulk at any price in lives – no matter how steep – to achieve their aims. To them, it is a matter of faith. They are the worshippers and servants of the Omnissiah, and to him is due all of the cold, hard information in the galaxy. The Adeptus Mechanicus will stoop to any means, no matter how cruel or underhanded, to offer up fresh knowledge to the Machine God.

Many amongst the Adeptus Mechanicus see a holy trinity within their deity, the third aspect of which is known as the Motive Force. This is the electrical energy present in living beings and machines both, an animating spark that emanates from, and belongs ultimately to, the Omnissiah. To the Tech-Priests Manipulus this is the most sacred and vital power in the universe, and one that it is their duty and their right to give and take as they see fit. The snaking mechadendrites of these figures can leech the Motive Force from anything they touch, or can release surging blasts of it into the Omnissiah's faithful in order to drive them into a fanatical war-fervour. The Tech-Priests Manipulus often lead Adeptus Mechanicus kill teams deep into enemy territory, the better to steal the energies of the foe.

Then there are the war-priests of the Machine Cult's congregations – the Electro-Priests of the Fulgurite and Corpuscarii sub-sects. These strange holy men have had their bodies wired with subcutaneous circuitry, allowing them to better siphon and channel the Motive Force, and are often deployed as elite kill teams by higher-ranking Tech-Priests when a vital mission must be completed in the Omnissiah's name.

Fulgurite Electro-Priests rip the Motive Force from their foes and bind it within themselves. They close with their enemies and belabour them with their electroleech staves, which leave machines and living beings alike drained, cold and inert. By comparison, Corpuscarii Electro-Priests seek to share the Motive Force with their enemies. Chanting rites of conductivity, they work themselves into a religious ecstasy before unleashing coruscating blasts of electricity that burn their victims alive from the inside out, and reduce enemy war machines to blackened and blazing husks.

Though the Fulgurites and Corpuscarii may be rival factions, they will set their differences aside when commanded to by a senior Tech-Priest. After all, the quest to recover the sacred mysteries of the Omnissiah from an ignorant galaxy must always be considered paramount.

ADEPTUS MECHANICUS KILL TEAMS

If every model in your kill team has the Adeptus Mechanicus Faction keyword, you can use Adeptus Mechanicus Tactics.

INFILTRATORS

Adeptus Mechanicus Tactic

Use this Tactic at the end of the Movement phase. Choose up to three **Sicarian Infiltrator** models from your kill team that were set up in Reserve and set them up anywhere on the battlefield that is more than 5" away from any enemy models.

1 COMMAND POINT

ADEPTUS MECHANICUS

MODEL	POINTS PER MODEL
Tech-Priest Manipulus (Level 1)	102
Tech-Priest Manipulus (Level 2)	122
Tech-Priest Manipulus (Level 3)	142
Tech-Priest Manipulus (Level 4)	167
WARGEAR	**POINTS PER ITEM**
Omnissian staff	0
Mechadendrites	0
Magnarail lance	0
Transonic cannon	10

GALVANIC PULSE

Adeptus Mechanicus Tactic
Tech-Priest Manipulus Aura Tactic

Use this Tactic at the start of the Movement phase if your kill team includes a **Tech-Priest Manipulus**. That model gains the following aura ability until the end of the battle round:

As long as this model is not shaken, you can add 1 to all Move characteristics for friendly models that begin your turn in the Movement phase within 6" of this model.

1 COMMAND POINT

TECH-PRIEST MANIPULUS

NAME	M	WS	BS	S	T	W	A	Ld	Sv	Max
Tech-Priest Manipulus	6"	3+	3+	4	4	4	3	8	2+	1

This model is armed with a magnarail lance, an Omnissian staff and mechadendrites.

WEAPON	RANGE	TYPE	S	AP	D	ABILITIES
Magnarail lance	18"	Heavy 1	7	-3	D3	When the bearer makes a shooting attack with this weapon in the Shooting phase, increase that attack's Damage characteristic to 3 if they remained stationary during the previous Movement phase.
Transonic cannon	8"	Assault D6	4	-1	2	This weapon automatically hits its target.
Omnissian staff	Melee	Melee	+2	-1	2	-
Mechadendrites	Melee	Melee	User	0	1	Each time the bearer fights, they may make D6 additional attacks with this weapon.

WARGEAR OPTIONS	• This model may replace its magnarail lance with a transonic cannon.
ABILITIES	**Canticles of the Omnissiah** (see the *Kill Team Core Manual*)
	Blessed Bionics: This model has a 5+ invulnerable save. In addition, at the beginning of each battle round, this model regains D3 lost wounds.
SPECIALISTS	**Fortitude, Leadership, Logistics, Shooting, Strategist, Strength**
FACTION KEYWORD	**Adeptus Mechanicus**
KEYWORDS	**Imperium, Cult Mechanicus, Commander, Infantry, Tech-Priest, Manipulus**

CORPUSCARII ELECTRO-PRIEST

NAME	M	WS	BS	S	T	W	A	Ld	Sv	Max
Corpuscarii Electro-Priest	6"	4+	3+	3	3	1	2	8	6+	-

This model is armed with electrostatic gauntlets.

ABILITIES	**Canticles of the Omnissiah** (see the *Kill Team Core Manual*) **Voltagheist Field:** This model has a 5+ invulnerable save. When this model finishes a charge move within 1" of an enemy model, pick an enemy model within 1" and roll a D6. On a roll of 6 the enemy model suffers a mortal wound.	**Fanatical Devotion:** Each time a model with this ability loses a wound, roll a D6; on a 5+ the model does not lose that wound. **Vision of the Motive Force:** This model's shooting attacks do not suffer any penalty to their hit rolls for the target model being obscured.
SPECIALISTS	Leader, Combat, Medic, Scout, Veteran, Zealot	
FACTION KEYWORD	ADEPTUS MECHANICUS	
KEYWORDS	IMPERIUM, CULT MECHANICUS, INFANTRY, ELECTRO-PRIEST, CORPUSCARII	

FULGURITE ELECTRO-PRIEST

NAME	M	WS	BS	S	T	W	A	Ld	Sv	Max
Fulgurite Electro-Priest	6"	3+	4+	3	3	1	2	8	6+	-

This model is armed with an electroleech stave.

ABILITIES	**Canticles of the Omnissiah** (see the *Kill Team Core Manual*) **Voltagheist Field:** This model has a 5+ invulnerable save. When this model finishes a charge move within 1" of an enemy model, pick an enemy model within 1" and roll a D6. On a roll of 6 the enemy model suffers a mortal wound.	**Fanatical Devotion:** Each time a model with this ability loses a wound, roll a D6; on a 5+ the model does not lose that wound. **Siphoned Vigour:** If this model takes an enemy model out of action in the Fight phase, its invulnerable save is improved to 3+ for the remainder of the mission.
SPECIALISTS	Leader, Combat, Medic, Scout, Veteran, Zealot	
FACTION KEYWORD	ADEPTUS MECHANICUS	
KEYWORDS	IMPERIUM, CULT MECHANICUS, INFANTRY, ELECTRO-PRIEST, FULGURITE	

RANGED WEAPONS

WEAPON	RANGE	TYPE	S	AP	D	ABILITIES
Electrostatic gauntlets	This weapon can be used as a ranged weapon and a melee weapon. When making shooting attacks or firing Overwatch with this weapon, use the ranged profile; when making close combat attacks, use the melee profile.					
- Ranged	12"	Assault 3	5	0	1	Each unmodified hit roll of 6 made for an attack with this weapon scores 3 hits rather than 1.
- Melee	Melee	Melee	5	0	1	

MELEE WEAPONS

WEAPON	RANGE	TYPE	S	AP	D	ABILITIES
Electroleech stave	Melee	Melee	+2	-2	D3	For each wound roll of 6+ for attacks with this weapon, the target suffers D3 mortal wounds instead of the normal damage.

KILL TEAM

MODEL	POINTS PER MODEL (Does not include wargear)
Corpuscarii Electro-Priest	13
Fulgurite Electro-Priest	14

MELEE WEAPONS

WEAPON	POINTS PER WEAPON
Electroleech stave	0

RANGED WEAPONS

WEAPON	POINTS PER WEAPON
Electrostatic gauntlets	0

ADEPTUS CUSTODES

Wise foes flee at the mere sight of the Adeptus Custodes' approach. During the glorious days of the Great Crusade these heroes fought at the side of the Emperor himself. After his fall they became his protectors and agents both, defending the Golden Throne and enforcing its inviolate will.

Nobility and power radiate from the warriors of the Adeptus Custodes. They are golden-armoured paragons of martial might and absolute incorruptibility, the solemn fury of the Emperor made manifest. Where they tread the enemies of Mankind know naught but defeat and despair. Clad in nigh-impenetrable auramite armour, wielding blades and firearms fashioned by the most skilled artificers of Holy Terra, the Adeptus Custodes are amongst the best-equipped warriors in the galaxy. Though what truly sets these champions apart is the genetic alchemy that goes into their creation. The Adeptus Custodes bear the spark of the Emperor's own divinity, their flesh and souls alike singing with such incredible power that a single Custodian can tear a Heretic Astartes warrior limb from limb with his bare hands, and lay low entire enemy warbands in the time it takes his victims to realise they are under attack.

Every member of the Adeptus Custodes is a hero in his own right. The Custodian Guard are exemplars all of their bloody craft, and whether hammering their enemies with hails of bolt fire or hacking them apart at close quarters, they can be relied upon to complete their mission no matter the odds. The Terminator-armoured Allarus Custodians are more fearsome still, for their unique mark of reinforced battle plate and their bellicose spirit enable them to perform deeds of spectacular heroism and violence. Meanwhile the Shield-Captains, who lead these brotherhoods into battle, are famed for their martial might and strategic wisdom both.

D6	BACKGROUND: HEROES' TALE
1	**Into the Stars:** This band of warriors have newly set out upon a mission of utmost importance.
2	**The Shadowed Hand:** These Custodes travel in secrecy, their mission classified at the highest level.
3	**Old Comrades:** In days gone by these warriors fought together to great effect. Now they are reunited in battle once more.
4	**Sworn to an Oath:** A quest of dire import must be completed before these warriors see Terra again.
5	**For Vengeance:** Originally part of a larger Shield Company, these surviving brothers will avenge the fall of their comrades no matter the cost.
6	**Earning Names:** These brave warriors are locked in fraternal competition, seeking not only to enact the Emperor's will, but to outdo one another's mighty deeds in the process.

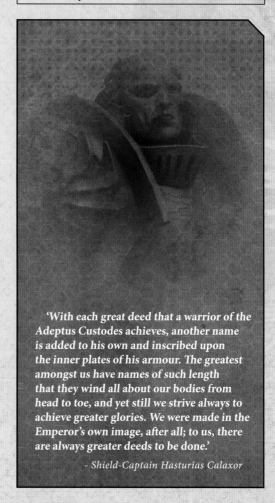

D6	MISSION: DUTY TO THE THRONE
1	**The Emperor's Blade:** A dangerous demagogue or enemy leader must be made an example of as though by the Emperor's own hand.
2	**Annihilation:** Those who pose a threat to Terra must be utterly destroyed.
3	**Secure and Shroud:** A dangerous artefact or tainted being must be snatched up and returned to the oubliettes hidden beneath the Imperial Palace.
4	**Vox Imperator:** The Custodes bear the holy word of the Emperor. It must reach its intended recipient.
5	**The Golden Shield:** Psychic augury indicates that an individual will serve the Golden Throne in some crucial fashion. They must be protected.
6	**Eyes of the Emperor:** Dark deeds are afoot that may endanger the throneworld itself. Information must be gathered and a warning swiftly dispatched.

'With each great deed that a warrior of the Adeptus Custodes achieves, another name is added to his own and inscribed upon the inner plates of his armour. The greatest amongst us have names of such length that they wind all about our bodies from head to toe, and yet still we strive always to achieve greater glories. We were made in the Emperor's own image, after all; to us, there are always greater deeds to be done.'

- Shield-Captain Hasturias Calaxor

The Adeptus Custodes are possessed of indomitable might and an absolute purity of will. No foul servant of the Dark Gods can stand against them, for they are the glory of the Emperor made manifest.

D10 SPECIALISTS' DEMEANOURS

1	**Bellicose:** This warrior is a ferocious fighter who approaches every battle head-on.
2	**Venerable:** This warrior has lived for more than a thousand years. There is little he has not seen before, and even less with the capacity to surprise him.
3	**Blood Games Victor:** To test the defences of the Golden Throne, Custodians launch mock strikes at it. Those who have won such Blood Games are skilled indeed.
4	**Xenophobe:** Having purged xenocults from the bowels of Terra itself, this warrior's hatred for aliens is absolute.
5	**True Hero:** So inspiring is this Custodian that no true Imperial servant can help but be stirred by his presence.
6	**Blademaster:** In close-quarters combat this warrior is utterly unstoppable.
7	**Stoic Shield:** This warrior stood amongst the Companion Guard of the Golden Throne itself. He is the master of the long vigil and the immovable defence.
8	**Unscrupulous:** Only the mission matters to this warrior, no matter how cruel or distasteful the means to achieve it.
9	**Grim Warden:** This warrior has long guarded the darkest secrets hidden beneath the Imperial palace. He fears nothing.
10	**Master Tactician:** So long has this warrior fought in the Emperor's service that he has gained a masterful grasp of battlefield tactics on every scale.

ADEPTUS CUSTODES NAME GENERATOR TABLE

D10	FORENAME	SURNAME
1	Tybalus	Constor
2	Yorta'kar	Gallimadean
3	Jaeharl	Drund
4	Tauramacchis	Talorn
5	Tristraen	Castivar
6	Sanash	Desh
7	Pydoris	Calaxor
8	Hasturian	Ghau
9	Nicodemus	Desmodages
10	Tybaris	Maxin

D6 SQUAD QUIRK: DEEPER WISDOMS

1	**Bane of Traitors:** This band of warriors detest the followers of Chaos with a particular fervour, and specialise in their annihilation.
2	**Vigilant:** Nothing escapes the notice of these Custodians, no matter how subtle or small.
3	**Loremasters:** This band of warriors prize knowledge highly and possess great stores of it, both esoteric and mundane.
4	**Shieldwar:** These warriors excel in turning the foe's advantages against them, and are at their most dangerous when outnumbered and outgunned.
5	**Famed:** The adventurous exploits of this warrior band are well known to their comrades, and they strive always to live up to their legend.
6	**Enforcers:** These Custodians see themselves as the enforcers of the Emperor's rule, and are accordingly grim and merciless in their conduct.

ADEPTUS CUSTODES KILL TEAMS

If every model in your kill team has the ADEPTUS CUSTODES Faction keyword, models in your kill team gain The Emperor's Chosen ability below, and you can use Adeptus Custodes Tactics.

The Emperor's Chosen: This model's invulnerable save is improved by 1 (to a maximum of 3+).

Adeptus Custodes Kill Team: An Adeptus Custodes kill team can be Battle-forged if it consists of at least two models (rather than three models), as long as it adheres to the other conditions set out in the *Kill Team Core Manual* (as modified by the mission, where relevant).

EVER VIGILANT

Adeptus Custodes Tactic

Use this Tactic at the end of the Movement phase when an opponent sets up a model within 12" of a model from your kill team that is not shaken. Your model can immediately shoot at the enemy model as if it were the Shooting phase, but you must subtract 1 from the resulting hit rolls.

2 COMMAND POINTS

INSPIRE FEAR

Adeptus Custodes Tactic

Use this Tactic at the beginning of the Morale phase. Choose a model from your kill team that is not shaken. Opponents must add 1 to Nerve tests taken for enemy models within 3" of that model in this phase.

1 COMMAND POINT

FROM GOLDEN LIGHT

Adeptus Custodes Tactic

Use this Tactic at the end of the Movement phase. Choose up to three TERMINATOR models from your kill team that were set up in Reserve and set them up anywhere on the battlefield that is more than 5" away from any enemy models.

1 COMMAND POINT

UNFLINCHING

Adeptus Custodes Tactic

Use this Tactic when an opponent chooses a model from your kill team that is not shaken as a target of a charge. When that model fires Overwatch in this phase, they successfully hit on a roll of 5 or 6.

1 COMMAND POINT

SPARK OF DIVINITY

Adeptus Custodes Tactic

Use this Tactic when an enemy PSYKER manifests a psychic power within 12" of a model from your kill team that is not shaken. You can take a Deny the Witch test for that model as if it were a PSYKER.

1 COMMAND POINT

CONCUSSION GRENADES

Adeptus Custodes Tactic

Use this Tactic when you choose an ALLARUS CUSTODIAN from your kill team to shoot with a balistus grenade launcher in the Shooting phase. Until the end of the battle round, that weapon has an AP characteristic of 0, but models that suffer any hits from that weapon cannot attack in the Shooting phase and your opponent must subtract 1 from hit rolls made for those models in the Fight phase.

1 COMMAND POINT

SHIELD-CAPTAIN

NAME	M	WS	BS	S	T	W	A	Ld	Sv	Max
Shield-Captain	6"	2+	2+	5	5	6	5	9	2+	1

This model is armed with a guardian spear.

WARGEAR OPTIONS	• This model may replace its guardian spear with a sentinel blade or castellan axe. • This model may take a misericordia. • If this model is armed with a sentinel blade, it may take a storm shield.
ABILITIES	**Aegis of the Emperor:** This model has a 5+ invulnerable save. In addition, roll a D6 each time a model with this ability suffers a mortal wound in the Psychic phase. On a 6 that mortal wound is ignored. **Superior Transhuman Physiology:** Ignore the penalty to this model's hit rolls from flesh wounds. **Storm Shield:** If this model is armed with a storm shield, it has a 3+ invulnerable save instead of a 5+ invulnerable save.
SPECIALISTS	Ferocity, Fortitude, Leadership, Logistics, Melee, Shooting, Stealth, Strategist, Strength
FACTION KEYWORD	ADEPTUS CUSTODES
KEYWORDS	IMPERIUM, COMMANDER, INFANTRY, SHIELD-CAPTAIN

INSPIRATIONAL FIGHTER

Adeptus Custodes Tactic
Shield-Captain Aura Tactic

Use this Tactic at the start of the Fight phase if your kill team includes a **SHIELD-CAPTAIN**. That model gains the following aura ability until the end of the battle round:

As long as this model is not shaken, you can re-roll hit rolls of 1 for friendly models within 6" of this model.

1 COMMAND POINT

ADEPTUS CUSTODES

MODEL	POINTS PER MODEL
Shield-Captain (Level 1)	118
Shield-Captain (Level 2)	138
Shield-Captain (Level 3)	158
Shield-Captain (Level 4)	183

WARGEAR	POINTS PER ITEM
Castellan axe	0
Guardian spear	0
Misericordia	2
Sentinel blade	0
Storm shield	15

CUSTODIAN GUARD

NAME	M	WS	BS	S	T	W	A	Ld	Sv	Max
Custodian Guard	6"	2+	2+	5	5	3	3	8	2+	-

This model is armed with a guardian spear.

WARGEAR OPTIONS	• This model may replace its guardian spear with a sentinel blade and storm shield. • This model may take a misericordia.

ABILITIES	**Aegis of the Emperor:** This model has a 5+ invulnerable save. In addition, roll a D6 each time a model with this ability suffers a mortal wound in the Psychic phase. On a 6 that mortal wound is ignored.	**Superior Transhuman Physiology:** Ignore the penalty to this model's hit rolls from flesh wounds. **Storm Shield:** If this model is armed with a storm shield, it has a 3+ invulnerable save instead of a 5+ invulnerable save.

SPECIALISTS	Leader, Combat, Scout, Sniper, Veteran, Zealot
FACTION KEYWORD	**ADEPTUS CUSTODES**
KEYWORDS	IMPERIUM, INFANTRY, CUSTODIAN GUARD

ALLARUS CUSTODIAN

NAME	M	WS	BS	S	T	W	A	Ld	Sv	Max
Allarus Custodian	6"	2+	2+	5	5	4	4	9	2+	-

This model is armed with a castellan axe and a balistus grenade launcher.

WARGEAR OPTIONS	• This model may replace its castellan axe with a guardian spear. • This model may take a misericordia.

ABILITIES	**Aegis of the Emperor:** This model has a 5+ invulnerable save. In addition, roll a D6 each time a model with this ability suffers a mortal wound in the Psychic phase. On a 6 that mortal wound is ignored. **Superior Transhuman Physiology:** Ignore the penalty to this model's hit rolls from flesh wounds.	**Slayer of Tyrants:** When this model piles in and consolidates, they can move up to 3" towards the nearest enemy Leader or **COMMANDER** even if it is not the nearest enemy model, so long as they finish this move within 1" of an enemy model.

SPECIALISTS	Leader, Combat, Demolitions, Sniper, Veteran, Zealot
FACTION KEYWORD	**ADEPTUS CUSTODES**
KEYWORDS	IMPERIUM, INFANTRY, TERMINATOR, ALLARUS CUSTODIAN

RANGED WEAPONS

WEAPON	RANGE	TYPE	S	AP	D	ABILITIES
Balistus grenade launcher	12"	Assault D3	4	-3	1	-
Castellan axe	This weapon can be used as a ranged weapon and a melee weapon. When making shooting attacks or firing Overwatch with this weapon, use the ranged profile; when making close combat attacks, use the melee profile.					
- Ranged	24"	Rapid Fire 1	4	-1	2	-
- Melee	Melee	Melee	+3	-2	D3	-
Guardian spear	This weapon can be used as a ranged weapon and a melee weapon. When making shooting attacks or firing Overwatch with this weapon, use the ranged profile; when making close combat attacks, use the melee profile.					
- Ranged	24"	Rapid Fire 1	4	-1	2	-
- Melee	Melee	Melee	+1	-3	D3	-
Sentinel blade	This weapon can be used as a ranged weapon and a melee weapon. When making shooting attacks or firing Overwatch with this weapon, use the ranged profile; when making close combat attacks, use the melee profile.					
- Ranged	12"	Pistol 2	4	0	1	-
- Melee	Melee	Melee	User	-3	D3	-

MELEE WEAPONS

WEAPON	RANGE	TYPE	S	AP	D	ABILITIES
Misericordia	Melee	Melee	User	-2	1	Each time the bearer fights, it can make 1 additional attack with this weapon unless it is also equipped with a storm shield.

KILL TEAM

MODEL	POINTS PER MODEL (Does not include wargear)
Allarus Custodian	67
Custodian Guard	33

RANGED WEAPONS

WEAPON	POINTS PER WEAPON
Balistus grenade launcher	0
Castellan axe	0
Guardian spear	0
Sentinel blade	0

MELEE WEAPONS

WEAPON	POINTS PER WEAPON
Misericordia	0

OTHER WARGEAR

WARGEAR	POINTS PER ITEM
Storm shield	0

ASTRA MILITARUM

The soldiers of the Astra Militarum make up the vast bulk of the Imperial war machine. It is they who lay down their lives on every battlefront to hold the line against tides of mutants, monsters and heretics. Yet even amongst the tragically expendable masses of the Imperial Guard, there are elite warriors that stand ready to deploy.

The greatest and most iconic strengths of the Astra Militarum lie in its practically inexhaustible masses of infantry and its vast reserves of armour and artillery. It is with these blunt instruments that the commanding officers of the Imperial Guard soak up the ferocity of their enemies' assaults and bludgeon their defences to ruin. It is true to form, then, that even the elite operatives of the Astra Militarum's kill teams are more concerned with destroying their enemies through brute force than through finesse.

Ogryns belong to one of the many divergent subspecies of Humanity known collectively as abhumans. They derive from high-gravity worlds where their physiologies have become ever more brutish and massive to compensate for the crushing conditions. So huge and strong is the average Ogryn that he can crumple a boltgun in one huge fist, soak up volleys of small arms fire without falling, and bludgeon his way through a ferrocrete wall using only his bare hands.

These hulking warriors are not especially intelligent, typically displaying a mental capacity well below that of their human comrades. However, providing they are well led and clearly directed, their stupendous strength and resilience allow them to smash a path through even the stoutest enemy defences.

Owing to their predilection for recklessly firing off all their ammunition in a few noisy and inaccurate bursts, Ogryns are armed with ripper guns. These weapons' huge drum magazines and burst limiters – not to mention their frighteningly large calibre – allow the Ogryns to make some meaningful ballistic contribution to most engagements, and if all else fails they can be wielded as devastatingly effective clubs.

Bullgryns are Ogryns trained and equipped for close assault and suppression operations. Clad in heavier armour than normal Ogryns and provided with an array of bulky metal shields, Bullgryns advance at a steady march while absorbing and deflecting overwhelming storms of enemy fire. Once they close on their foes, Bullgryns hammer them with explosive volleys from their grenadier gauntlets, or charge headlong into combat and lay about themselves with massive maces. Though far from subtle, a kill team of Bullgryns can be pointed in a direction and relied upon to ruin any enemy assets, inconvenient architecture and unfortunate passers-by that may stand between them and their commander's objective. It is a talent that the Astra Militarum prizes highly.

Abhumans are far from the only specialist troops available to the Astra Militarum, of course. Many veteran soldiers fight amongst the ranks of the Imperial Guard. Perhaps the most infamous and feared of all of these is the Catachan one-man-army known as Sly Marbo. His legend tells of ten brothers who were sent into battle upon an unnamed world, and of the single, hollow-eyed survivor who returned to fight an endless war of vengeance for his fallen kin. Marbo comes and goes as he pleases, a ghost of the jungles who accepts each mission with a cold – almost vacant – stare then sets off to wreak slaughter.

Marbo fights like a Daemon, shredding enemies with his ripper pistol, his vicious Catachan fang and a preternatural talent for ambush warfare and explosives. He has massacred entire kill teams single-handed, and his crusade of violence shows no signs of ending.

ASTRA MILITARUM KILL TEAMS

If every model in your kill team has the ASTRA MILITARUM Faction keyword, you can use Astra Militarum Tactics.

AERIAL DROP

Astra Militarum Tactic

Use this Tactic at the end of the Movement phase. Choose up to three models that are any combination of **MILITARUM TEMPESTUS SCION** and/or **TEMPESTOR PRIME** models from your kill team that were set up in Reserve and set them up anywhere on the battlefield that is more than 5" away from any enemy models.

1 COMMAND POINT

SLY MARBO

NAME	M	WS	BS	S	T	W	A	Ld	Sv	Max
Sly Marbo	6"	2+	2+	3	3	4	4	7	5+	1

This model is armed with a ripper pistol, envenomed blade and frag grenades.
Only one of this model may be included on your command roster.

WEAPON	RANGE	TYPE	S	AP	D	ABILITIES
Ripper pistol	12"	Pistol 3	5	0	1	This weapon wounds on a 2+.
Envenomed blade	Melee	Melee	+1	0	1	This weapon wounds on a 2+.

ABILITIES	
	Loner: The Voice of Command ability has no effect on Sly Marbo.
	Lethal Ambush: When you set up Sly Marbo from Reserve, you may choose one of the following:
	• **Stalk with Blade:** You can immediately declare that Sly Marbo will attempt to charge, though you may only roll a single D6 (rather than 2D6) for the charge roll. In addition, until the end of the battle round, add 2 to Sly Marbo's Attacks characteristic.
	• **Snipe with Pistol:** Sly Marbo can immediately shoot his ripper pistol as if it were the Shooting phase.
	• **Detonate Concealed Explosives:** Roll a D6 for each of up to 6 enemy models on the battlefield. On a 6 the model being rolled for and all models within 2" of that model suffer a mortal wound.

SPECIALISTS	Legendary Hunter (Level 4)
FACTION KEYWORD	**ASTRA MILITARUM**
KEYWORDS	**IMPERIUM, COMMANDER, INFANTRY, SLY MARBO**

KNIFE IN THE DARK

Astra Militarum Tactic
Sly Marbo Tactic

Use this Tactic in the Fight phase when Sly Marbo makes an attack, but before making the hit roll. If the attack hits, the target suffers D3 mortal wounds and the attack sequence ends.

2 COMMAND POINTS

ASTRA MILITARUM

MODEL	POINTS PER MODEL
Sly Marbo (Level 4)	55
WARGEAR	**POINTS PER ITEM**
Envenomed blade	0
Frag grenades	0
Ripper pistol	0

OGRYN

NAME	M	WS	BS	S	T	W	A	Ld	Sv	Max
Ogryn	6"	3+	4+	5	5	3	3	7	5+	-
Ogryn Bone 'ead	6"	3+	4+	5	5	3	4	8	5+	1

This model is armed with a ripper gun and frag bombs.
One Ogryn in your kill team can be an Ogryn Bone 'ead.

ABILITIES	**Avalanche of Muscle:** You can add 1 to the Attacks characteristic of this model in the Fight phase of any battle round in which it charged. This ability may only be used the first time this model fights each battle round.
SPECIALISTS	**Leader** (Bone 'ead only), **Combat**, **Demolitions**, **Heavy**, **Veteran**
FACTION KEYWORD	**ASTRA MILITARUM**
KEYWORDS	**IMPERIUM, MILITARUM AUXILLA, INFANTRY, OGRYN**

BULLGRYN

NAME	M	WS	BS	S	T	W	A	Ld	Sv	Max
Bullgryn	6"	3+	4+	5	5	3	3	7	4+	-
Bullgryn Bone 'ead	6"	3+	4+	5	5	3	4	8	4+	1

This model is armed with a grenadier gauntlet, frag bombs and a slabshield.
One Bullgryn in your kill team can be a Bullgryn Bone 'ead.

WARGEAR OPTIONS	• This model may replace its grenadier gauntlet with a Bullgryn maul. • This model may replace its slabshield with a brute shield.
ABILITIES	**Avalanche of Muscle:** You can add 1 to the Attacks characteristic of this model in the Fight phase of any battle round in which it charged. This ability may only be used the first time this model fights each battle round. **Brute Shield:** A model with a brute shield has a 4+ invulnerable save. **Slabshield:** Add 2 to saving throws made against attacks that target a model with a slab shield.
SPECIALISTS	**Leader** (Bone 'ead only), **Combat**, **Demolitions**, **Heavy**, **Veteran**
FACTION KEYWORD	**ASTRA MILITARUM**
KEYWORDS	**IMPERIUM, MILITARUM AUXILLA, INFANTRY, OGRYN, BULLGRYN**

RANGED WEAPONS

WEAPON	RANGE	TYPE	S	AP	D	ABILITIES
Frag bomb	6"	Grenade D6	4	0	1	-
Grenadier gauntlet	12"	Assault D6	4	0	1	-
Ripper gun		This weapon can be used as a ranged weapon and a melee weapon. When making shooting attacks or firing Overwatch with this weapon, use the ranged profile; when making close combat attacks, use the melee profile.				
- Ranged	12"	Assault 3	5	0	1	-
- Melee	Melee	Melee	User	-1	1	-

MELEE WEAPONS

WEAPON	RANGE	TYPE	S	AP	D	ABILITIES
Bullgryn maul	Melee	Melee	+2	-1	2	-

KILL TEAM

MODEL	POINTS PER MODEL (Does not include wargear)
Bullgryn	37
- Bullgryn Bone 'ead	38
Ogryn	26
- Ogryn Bone 'ead	27

RANGED WEAPONS

WEAPON	POINTS PER WEAPON
Frag bombs	0
Grenadier gauntlet	0
Ripper gun	0

MELEE WEAPONS

WEAPON	POINTS PER WEAPON
Bullgryn maul	2

OTHER WARGEAR

WARGEAR	POINTS PER ITEM
Brute shield	0
Slabshield	3

HERETIC ASTARTES

Sworn enemies of the Imperium and traitors to the Emperor's rule, the Heretic Astartes are Space Marines who have fallen to the dark temptations of Chaos. They are anathema to everything they once stood for, tainted champions who fight for the favour of the Dark Gods and the powerful rewards those fell entities can bestow.

The Chaos Space Marines are amongst the deadliest foes faced by the Imperium. Their might is equal to that of the Adeptus Astartes, but is bolstered further by the gifts of the Dark Gods. Strange psychic powers, foul mutations and daemonically empowered weapons are common amongst their traitorous ranks, allowing them to rend apart their victims with contemptuous ease or even sever their very souls from their bodies.

From fanatical Cultists to formidable renegade Space Marines, the Dark Gods do not want for deadly servants to enact their wills. However, when the most crucial of missions must be completed or the vilest deeds performed, specialist operatives and monstrous warrior-lords form chosen kill teams to see them done.

Clad in baroque Terminator armour that has been warped and twisted by the energies of Chaos, Lords and Sorcerers stride into battle with the arrogant confidence of demigods of ruin. They wield fearsome Daemon-blades and unleash reality-twisting powers that reduce their enemies to gibbering Chaos Spawn or mangled corpses. Dark Apostles bellow praise to the Dark Gods, spitting heretical sermons and sanity-flaying curses into their enemies' faces before bludgeoning them to death with tainted croziuses. Masters of Executions hunt their quarry across the battlefield, brutally butchering and making an example of those who have angered the lords of the Heretic Astartes, while Masters of Possession use their infernal powers to taint vital cogitator engines, force daemonic possession upon enemy commanders and empower their Chaos Space Marine brethren with the unnatural might to overcome any foe.

Bands of Chaos Terminators make for exceptional kill teams, teleporting directly into the heart of their enemies' defences to open the way for full-scale invasion or strike down those who believe themselves safe from the Dark Gods' wrath. With their hulking armour and unnatural resilience, they can endure punishment that would reduce entire regiments of lesser warriors to bloody ruin. At the same time, the Terminators unleash ferocious firepower of their own to blow crucial targets apart, reduce libraries of irreplaceable lore to ash and gun down the foe's greatest champions. Any who survive the first fusillade fall soon enough, bisected by crackling power blades or crushed by clawed power fists.

Then there are those Heretic Astartes who embrace power in exchange for damnation. Khorne Berzerkers have cast aside sanity and reason to wreak endless slaughter in the Blood God's name. Meanwhile, opening themselves up to Daemons, Possessed and Greater Possessed sacrifice body and soul that their flesh might be moulded into a living weapon of the Dark Gods. Their limbs twist into chitinous blades and lashing tendrils, their faces into horrific visages of needle fangs and bulging compound eyes. Their bodies crackle with daemonic energy that can turn aside bolt and blade. The Possessed are powerful kill team operatives, but their shortcut to martial might has cost them everything.

HERETIC ASTARTES KILL TEAMS

If every model in your kill team has the HERETIC ASTARTES Faction keyword, you can use Heretic Astartes Tactics.

TELEPORT STRIKE

Heretic Astartes Tactic

Use this Tactic at the end of the Movement phase. Choose up to three TERMINATOR models from your kill team that were set up in Reserve and set them up anywhere on the battlefield that is more than 5" away from any enemy models.

1 COMMAND POINT

VETERANS OF THE LONG WAR

Heretic Astartes Tactic

Use this Tactic when a CHAOS SPACE MARINE or TERMINATOR model from your kill team is chosen to attack in the Shooting or Fight phase. You can add 1 to wound rolls for the model's attacks that target IMPERIUM models until the end of the phase.

2 COMMAND POINTS

GREATER POSSESSED

NAME	M	WS	BS	S	T	W	A	Ld	Sv	Max
Greater Possessed	7"	2+	3+	5	5	5	5	8	3+	1

This model is armed with daemonic mutations.

WEAPON	RANGE	TYPE	S	AP	D	ABILITIES
Daemonic mutations	Melee	Melee	User	-2	D3	-

ABILITIES	
	Death to the False Emperor: If a model with this ability makes an attack in the Fight phase which targets an IMPERIUM model, each time you make a hit roll of 6+ you may make an additional attack with the same weapon against the same target. These attacks cannot themselves generate any further attacks. **Transhuman Physiology:** Ignore the penalty to this model's hit rolls from one flesh wound it has suffered.	**Mark of Chaos:** When you add a model with the <MARK OF CHAOS> keyword to your kill team, you can choose to replace it with one of the following keywords: KHORNE, TZEENTCH, NURGLE or SLAANESH, or you can choose for it to have no mark. If you choose a mark, note this on the model's datacard. **Daemonic:** This model has a 5+ invulnerable save.
SPECIALISTS	Ferocity, Fortitude, Melee, Strength
FACTION KEYWORD	HERETIC ASTARTES
KEYWORDS	CHAOS, <MARK OF CHAOS>, COMMANDER, INFANTRY, DAEMON, GREATER POSSESSED

LOCUS OF POWER

Heretic Astartes Tactic
Greater Possessed Aura Tactic

Use this Tactic at the start of the Fight phase if your kill team includes a GREATER POSSESSED. That model gains the following aura ability until the end of the battle round:

As long as this model is not shaken, add 1 to the Strength characteristic of friendly DAEMON models within 6" of this model that share the KHORNE, TZEENTCH, NURGLE or SLAANESH keyword with this model.

1 COMMAND POINT

HERETIC ASTARTES

MODEL	POINTS PER MODEL
Greater Possessed (Level 1)	80
Greater Possessed (Level 2)	100
Greater Possessed (Level 3)	120
Greater Possessed (Level 4)	145
WARGEAR	**POINTS PER ITEM**
Daemonic mutations	0

MASTER OF EXECUTIONS

NAME	M	WS	BS	S	T	W	A	Ld	Sv	Max
Master of Executions	6"	2+	3+	4	4	4	4	8	3+	1

This model is armed with a bolt pistol, an axe of dismemberment, frag grenades and krak grenades.

WEAPON	RANGE	TYPE	S	AP	D	ABILITIES
Axe of dismemberment	Melee	Melee	x2	-3	D3	-

ABILITIES	**Death to the False Emperor:** If a model with this ability makes an attack in the Fight phase which targets an **IMPERIUM** model, each time you make a hit roll of 6+ you may make an additional attack with the same weapon against the same target. These attacks cannot themselves generate any further attacks. **Mark of Chaos:** When you add a model with the <**MARK OF CHAOS**> keyword to your kill team, you can choose to replace it with one of the following keywords: **KHORNE**, **TZEENTCH**, **NURGLE** or **SLAANESH**, or you can choose for it to have no mark. If you choose a mark, note this on the model's datacard. **Transhuman Physiology:** Ignore the penalty to this model's hit rolls from one flesh wound it has suffered. **Feared Headsman:** Your opponents must add 1 to Nerve tests taken for enemy models within 3" of any models (other than shaken models) with this ability. **Warp-sighted Butcher:** Re-roll failed wound rolls for attacks made by this model.
SPECIALISTS	**Ferocity, Fortitude, Melee, Strength**
FACTION KEYWORD	**HERETIC ASTARTES**
KEYWORDS	**CHAOS, <MARK OF CHAOS>, COMMANDER, INFANTRY, MASTER OF EXECUTIONS**

RITUAL SACRIFICE

Heretic Astartes Tactic
Master of Executions Tactic

Use this Tactic when a **MASTER OF EXECUTIONS** in your kill team takes an enemy model out of action with an attack in the Fight phase. Roll a D6. On a 2+, add 1 to the Master of Executions' Strength, Toughness, Wounds or Attacks (choose one).
You can only choose each characteristic once per mission, and the characteristic increase lasts until the end of the mission.

1 COMMAND POINT

HERETIC ASTARTES

MODEL	POINTS PER MODEL
Master of Executions (Level 1)	71
Master of Executions (Level 2)	91
Master of Executions (Level 3)	111
Master of Executions (Level 4)	136

WARGEAR	POINTS PER ITEM
Axe of dismemberment	0
Bolt pistol	0
Frag grenades	0
Krak grenades	0

DARK APOSTLE

NAME	M	WS	BS	S	T	W	A	Ld	Sv	Max
Dark Apostle	6"	2+	3+	4	4	4	3	9	3+	1
Dark Disciple	6"	4+	5+	3	3	1	1	6	5+	2

This model is armed with a power maul, bolt pistol, frag grenades and krak grenades.
If your kill team includes a Dark Apostle, it may include up to two Dark Disciples.

WARGEAR OPTIONS	• A Dark Apostle may replace its bolt pistol with a combi-bolter, combi-flamer, combi-melta, combi-plasma or plasma pistol.
ABILITIES	**Death to the False Emperor:** If a model with this ability makes an attack in the Fight phase which targets an **IMPERIUM** model, each time you make a hit roll of 6+ you may make an additional attack with the same weapon against the same target. These attacks cannot themselves generate any further attacks.
	Mark of Chaos: When you add a model with the <**MARK OF CHAOS**> keyword to your kill team, you can choose to replace it with one of the following keywords: **KHORNE**, **TZEENTCH**, **NURGLE** or **SLAANESH**, or you can choose for it to have no mark. If you choose a mark, note this on the model's datacard.
	Transhuman Physiology: Ignore the penalty to a Dark Apostle's hit rolls from one flesh wound it has suffered.
	Sigil of Corruption: A Dark Apostle has a 4+ invulnerable save.
	Followers: Models do not suffer any penalty to their Nerve tests for a friendly Dark Disciple being out of action. Dark Disciples cannot be specialists, are not part of a fire team and cannot gain experience.
	Relic of Corruption: Add 1" to the range of a Dark Apostle's Aura Tactics for each friendly Dark Disciple that is within 1" of that Dark Apostle.
SPECIALISTS	Ferocity, Fortitude, Leadership, Melee, Strength
FACTION KEYWORD	**HERETIC ASTARTES**
KEYWORDS	**CHAOS**, <**MARK OF CHAOS**>, **COMMANDER**, **INFANTRY**, **DARK APOSTLE** (Dark Disciple is **CHAOS**, <**MARK OF CHAOS**>, **INFANTRY**, **DARK DISCIPLE**)

DARK ZEALOTRY

Heretic Astartes Tactic
Dark Apostle Aura Tactic

Use this Tactic at the start of the Fight phase if your kill team includes a **DARK APOSTLE**. That model gains the following aura ability until the end of the battle round:

As long as this model is not shaken, you can re-roll failed hit rolls in the Fight phase for friendly models within 6" of this model.

1 COMMAND POINT

HERETIC ASTARTES

MODEL	POINTS PER MODEL
Dark Apostle (Level 1)	49
Dark Apostle (Level 2)	64
Dark Apostle (Level 3)	79
Dark Apostle (Level 4)	104
Dark Disciple	4

WARGEAR	POINTS PER ITEM
Bolt pistol	0
Combi-bolter	4
Combi-flamer	12
Combi-melta	14
Combi-plasma	12
Frag grenades	0
Krak grenades	0
Plasma pistol	4
Power maul	0

MASTER OF POSSESSION

NAME	M	WS	BS	S	T	W	A	Ld	Sv	Max
Master of Possession	6"	3+	3+	4	4	4	3	9	3+	1

This model is armed with a force stave, bolt pistol, frag grenades and krak grenades.

WEAPON	RANGE	TYPE	S	AP	D	ABILITIES
Force stave	Melee	Melee	+2	-1	D3	-

ABILITIES	**Death to the False Emperor:** If a model with this ability makes an attack in the Fight phase which targets an **IMPERIUM** model, each time you make a hit roll of 6+ you may make an additional attack with the same weapon against the same target. These attacks cannot themselves generate any further attacks.
	Mark of Chaos: When you add a model with the <**MARK OF CHAOS**> keyword to your kill team, you can choose to replace it with one of the following keywords: **TZEENTCH**, **NURGLE** or **SLAANESH**, or you can choose for it to have no mark. If you choose a mark, note this on the model's datacard.
	Rite of Possession: PSYKERS suffer Perils of the Warp on any Psychic test roll of a double that is made for them, instead of just double 1 or 6, while they are within 12" of any enemy models with this ability.
	Transhuman Physiology: Ignore the penalty to this model's hit rolls from one flesh wound it has suffered.
	Aura of Dark Glory: This model has a 5+ invulnerable save.
PSYKER	This model can attempt to manifest two psychic powers and deny one psychic power in each Psychic phase. It knows the *Psybolt* psychic power as well as two psychic powers generated from the Malefic discipline (see below).
SPECIALISTS	Fortitude, Leadership, Melee, Psyker, Strength
FACTION KEYWORD	**HERETIC ASTARTES**
KEYWORDS	**CHAOS**, <**MARK OF CHAOS**>, **COMMANDER**, **INFANTRY**, **PSYKER**, **MASTER OF POSSESSION**

MALEFIC DISCIPLINE

To generate psychic powers from the Malefic discipline, you can either roll a D3 to generate them randomly (re-roll any duplicate results), or you can select those you wish the psyker to have. Do so before each battle.

D3 RESULT

1 SACRIFICE

The psyker uses a sacrificial soul to remould and repair an unholy Daemon-form.

Sacrifice has a warp charge value of 4. If manifested, choose any model within 2" of the psyker; that model suffers a mortal wound. Then, choose a friendly **DAEMON** model within 12" of the psyker. Remove all flesh wounds from that model.

2 CURSED EARTH

The psyker becomes a conduit through which the energies of the warp flow, tainting the very ground and sustaining the Daemonkin that walk upon it.

Cursed Earth has a warp charge value of 7. If manifested, then until the start of the next psychic phase, the invulnerable save of friendly **DAEMON** models is improved by 1 (to a maximum of 3+) whilst they are within 6" of this psyker.

3 INFERNAL POWER

The fell power of the immaterium flows from the psyker, imbuing the Daemons that reside within his followers' bodies with even greater ferocity.

Infernal Power has a warp charge value of 6. If manifested, then until the start of the next Psychic phase re-roll hit and wound rolls of 1 for friendly **DAEMON** models whilst they are within 6" of this psyker.

HERETIC ASTARTES	
MODEL	**POINTS PER MODEL**
Master of Possession (Level 1)	68
Master of Possession (Level 2)	88
Master of Possession (Level 3)	108
Master of Possession (Level 4)	133
WARGEAR	**POINTS PER ITEM**
Bolt pistol	0
Force stave	0
Frag grenades	0
Krak grenades	0

SORCERER IN TERMINATOR ARMOUR

NAME	M	WS	BS	S	T	W	A	Ld	Sv	Max
Sorcerer in Terminator Armour	5"	3+	3+	4	4	5	3	9	2+	1

This model is armed with a force stave and combi-bolter.

WEAPON	RANGE	TYPE	S	AP	D	ABILITIES
Force axe	Melee	Melee	+1	-2	D3	-
Force stave	Melee	Melee	+2	-1	D3	-
Force sword	Melee	Melee	User	-3	D3	-

WARGEAR OPTIONS	• This model may replace its combi-bolter with a combi-flamer, combi-melta, combi-plasma, chainfist, lightning claw, power axe, power fist, power maul or power sword. • This model may replace its force stave with a force axe or force sword.
ABILITIES	**Death to the False Emperor:** If a model with this ability makes an attack in the Fight phase which targets an IMPERIUM model, each time you make a hit roll of 6+ you may make an additional attack with the same weapon against the same target. These attacks cannot themselves generate any further attacks. **Mark of Chaos:** When you add a model with the <MARK OF CHAOS> keyword to your kill team, you can choose to replace it with one of the following keywords: TZEENTCH, NURGLE or SLAANESH, or you can choose for it to have no mark. If you choose a mark, note this on the model's datacard. **Transhuman Physiology:** Ignore the penalty to this model's hit rolls from one flesh wound it has suffered. **Terminator Armour:** This model has a 5+ invulnerable save.
PSYKER	This model can attempt to manifest two psychic powers and deny one psychic power in each Psychic phase. It knows the *Psybolt* psychic power as well as two psychic powers generated from the Dark Hereticus discipline (see *Kill Team: Commanders*).
SPECIALISTS	**Fortitude, Melee, Psyker, Shooting, Strength**
FACTION KEYWORD	HERETIC ASTARTES
KEYWORDS	CHAOS, <MARK OF CHAOS>, COMMANDER, INFANTRY, TERMINATOR, PSYKER, SORCERER

HERETIC ASTARTES

MODEL	POINTS PER MODEL
Sorcerer in Terminator Armour (Level 1)	88
Sorcerer in Terminator Armour (Level 2)	108
Sorcerer in Terminator Armour (Level 3)	128
Sorcerer in Terminator Armour (Level 4)	153

WARGEAR	POINTS PER ITEM
Combi-bolter	0
Combi-flamer	8
Combi-melta	10
Combi-plasma	8
Chainfist	0
Force axe	2
Force stave	0
Force sword	0
Lightning claw	0
Power axe	0
Power fist	0
Power maul	0
Power sword	0

CHAOS LORD IN TERMINATOR ARMOUR

NAME	M	WS	BS	S	T	W	A	Ld	Sv	Max
Chaos Lord in Terminator Armour	5"	2+	2+	4	4	6	4	9	2+	1

This model is armed with a power sword and combi-bolter.

WARGEAR OPTIONS	• This model may replace its combi-bolter with a combi-flamer, combi-melta, combi-plasma, chainfist, lightning claw, power axe, power fist, power maul or power sword. • This model may replace its power sword with a chainfist, lightning claw, power axe, power fist or power maul.
ABILITIES	**Death to the False Emperor:** If a model with this ability makes an attack in the Fight phase which targets an **IMPERIUM** model, each time you make a hit roll of 6+ you may make an additional attack with the same weapon against the same target. These attacks cannot themselves generate any further attacks. **Mark of Chaos:** When you add a model with the <**MARK OF CHAOS**> keyword to your kill team, you can choose to replace it with one of the following keywords: **KHORNE, TZEENTCH, NURGLE** or **SLAANESH**, or you can choose for it to have no mark. If you choose a mark, note this on the model's datacard. **Transhuman Physiology:** Ignore the penalty to this model's hit rolls from one flesh wound it has suffered. **Sigil of Corruption:** This model has a 4+ invulnerable save.
SPECIALISTS	**Ferocity, Fortitude, Leadership, Logistics, Melee, Shooting, Strategist, Strength**
FACTION KEYWORD	**HERETIC ASTARTES**
KEYWORDS	**CHAOS, <MARK OF CHAOS>, COMMANDER, INFANTRY, TERMINATOR, CHAOS LORD**

LORD OF CHAOS

Heretic Astartes Tactic
Chaos Lord in Terminator Armour Aura Tactic

Use this Tactic at the start of the Shooting phase if your kill team includes a **TERMINATOR CHAOS LORD**. That model gains the following aura ability until the end of the battle round:

As long as this model is not shaken, you can re-roll hit rolls of 1 for friendly models within 6" of this model.

1 COMMAND POINT

HERETIC ASTARTES

MODEL	POINTS PER MODEL
Chaos Lord in Terminator Armour (Level 1)	80
Chaos Lord in Terminator Armour (Level 2)	100
Chaos Lord in Terminator Armour (Level 3)	120
Chaos Lord in Terminator Armour (Level 4)	145

WARGEAR	POINTS PER ITEM
Combi-bolter	0
Combi-flamer	8
Combi-melta	10
Combi-plasma	8
Chainfist	13
Lightning claw (single/pair)	4/8
Power axe	2
Power fist	12
Power maul	0
Power sword	0

KHORNE BERZERKER

NAME	M	WS	BS	S	T	W	A	Ld	Sv	Max
Khorne Berzerker	6"	3+	3+	5	4	1	2	7	3+	-
Berzerker Destroyer	6"	3+	3+	5	4	1	2	7	3+	2
Berzerker Champion	6"	3+	3+	5	4	1	3	8	3+	1

This model is armed with a chainsword, bolt pistol, frag grenades and krak grenades. Up to two Khorne Berzerkers in your kill team can be Berzerker Destroyers, and one Khorne Berzerker in your kill team can be a Berzerker Champion.

WARGEAR OPTIONS	• This model may replace its chainsword or bolt pistol with a chainaxe. • A Berzerker Destroyer may replace their bolt pistol with a plasma pistol. • A Berzerker Champion may replace their bolt pistol and chainsword with up to two weapons from the following list: bolt pistol, chainaxe, chainsword, lightning claw, plasma pistol, power axe, power fist, power maul or power sword. Alternatively, they may replace their bolt pistol and chainsword with up to one weapon from that list, and one weapon from the following list: boltgun, combi-bolter, combi-flamer, combi-melta or combi-plasma. • One Khorne Berzerker in your kill team may take an Icon of Wrath.
ABILITIES	**Death to the False Emperor:** If a model with this ability makes an attack in the Fight phase which targets an **IMPERIUM** model, each time you roll a hit roll of 6+ you may make an additional attack with the same weapon against the same target. These attacks cannot themselves generate any further attacks. **Transhuman Physiology:** Ignore the penalty to this model's hit rolls from one flesh wound it has suffered. **Blood for the Blood God:** In the Fight phase, after this model has fought in that phase for the first time, when it is your turn to pick a model to fight with later in the same phase, this model can be selected to fight for a second time if it is within 3" of any enemy models.
SPECIALISTS	**Leader** (Champion only), **Combat, Demolitions, Veteran, Zealot**
FACTION KEYWORD	**HERETIC ASTARTES**
KEYWORDS	**CHAOS, KHORNE, INFANTRY, KHORNE BERZERKER**

POSSESSED

NAME	M	WS	BS	S	T	W	A	Ld	Sv	Max
Possessed	7"	3+	3+	5	4	2	*	8	3+	-

This model is armed with horrifying mutations.

ABILITIES	**Death to the False Emperor:** If a model with this ability makes an attack in the Fight phase which targets an **IMPERIUM** model, each time you make a hit roll of 6+ you may make an additional attack with the same weapon against the same target. These attacks cannot themselves generate any further attacks. **Transhuman Physiology:** Ignore the penalty to this model's hit rolls from one flesh wound it has suffered. **Daemonic:** This model has a 5+ invulnerable save.	**Mark of Chaos:** When you add a model with the **<MARK OF CHAOS>** keyword to your kill team, you can choose to replace it with one of the following keywords: **KHORNE**, **TZEENTCH**, **NURGLE** or **SLAANESH**, or you can choose for it to have no mark. If you choose a mark, note this on the model's datacard. **Writhing Tentacles:** Roll a D3 when a this model is selected to attack in the Fight phase. The result is the Attacks characteristic of this model until the end of the phase.
SPECIALISTS	**Leader, Combat, Stealth, Veteran, Zealot**	
FACTION KEYWORD	**HERETIC ASTARTES**	
KEYWORDS	**CHAOS, <MARK OF CHAOS>, INFANTRY, DAEMON, POSSESSED**	

TERMINATOR

NAME	M	WS	BS	S	T	W	A	Ld	Sv	Max
Terminator	5"	3+	3+	4	4	2	2	8	2+	-
Terminator Gunner	5"	3+	3+	4	4	2	2	8	2+	2
Terminator Champion	5"	3+	3+	4	4	2	3	9	2+	1

This model is armed with a combi-bolter and chainaxe.
Up to two Terminators in your kill team can be Terminator Gunners, and one Terminator in your kill team can be a Terminator Champion.

WARGEAR OPTIONS	<ul><li>This model may replace its combi-bolter with a combi-flamer, combi-melta or combi-plasma.</li><li>This model may replace its chainaxe with a chainfist, lightning claw, power axe, power fist, power maul or power sword.</li><li>A Terminator Gunner may replace their combi-bolter with a combi-flamer, combi-melta, combi-plasma, heavy flamer or reaper autocannon.</li><li>A Terminator or Terminator Champion may replace their combi-bolter and chainaxe with a pair of lightning claws.</li><li>One Terminator in your kill team may take a Chaos Icon. If they have the **KHORNE**, **TZEENTCH**, **NURGLE** or **SLAANESH** keyword, they must have the appropriate Icon from the Chaos Icons listed in the *Kill Team Core Manual*. If they have no mark, they must take an Icon of Vengeance (see the *Kill Team Core Manual*).</li></ul>	
ABILITIES	**Death to the False Emperor:** If a model with this ability makes an attack in the Fight phase which targets an **IMPERIUM** model, each time you make a hit roll of 6+ you may make an additional attack with the same weapon against the same target. These attacks cannot themselves generate any further attacks. **Terminator Armour:** This model has a 5+ invulnerable save.	**Mark of Chaos:** When you add a model with the **<MARK OF CHAOS>** keyword to your kill team, you can choose to replace it with one of the following keywords: **KHORNE**, **TZEENTCH**, **NURGLE** or **SLAANESH**, or you can choose for it to have no mark. If you choose a mark, note this on the model's datacard. **Transhuman Physiology:** Ignore the penalty to this model's hit rolls from one flesh wound it has suffered.
SPECIALISTS	**Leader** (Champion only), **Heavy** (Gunner only), **Combat, Comms, Demolitions, Veteran**	
FACTION KEYWORD	**HERETIC ASTARTES**	
KEYWORDS	**CHAOS, <MARK OF CHAOS>, INFANTRY, TERMINATOR**	

RANGED WEAPONS

WEAPON	RANGE	TYPE	S	AP	D	ABILITIES
Combi-bolter	24"	Rapid Fire 2	4	0	1	-
Combi-flamer	When attacking with this weapon, choose one or both of the profiles below. If you choose both, subtract 1 from all hit rolls made for this weapon.					
- Boltgun	24"	Rapid Fire 1	4	0	1	-
- Flamer	8"	Assault D6	4	0	1	This weapon automatically hits its target.
Combi-melta	When attacking with this weapon, choose one or both of the profiles below. If you choose both, subtract 1 from all hit rolls made for this weapon.					
- Boltgun	24"	Rapid Fire 1	4	0	1	-
- Meltagun	12"	Assault 1	8	-4	D6	If the target is within half range of this weapon, roll two dice when inflicting damage with it and discard the lowest result.
Combi-plasma	When attacking with this weapon, choose one or both of the profiles below. If you choose both, subtract 1 from all hit rolls made for this weapon.					
- Boltgun	24"	Rapid Fire 1	4	0	1	-
- Plasma gun	24"	Rapid Fire 1	7	-3	1	This weapon can be supercharged by the bearer before firing. If they do so, increase the Strength and Damage of the weapon by 1 this turn. On any unmodified hit rolls of 1 when firing supercharge, the bearer is taken out of action after all of the weapon's shots have been resolved.
Heavy flamer	8"	Heavy D6	5	-1	1	This weapon automatically hits its target.
Reaper autocannon	36"	Heavy 4	7	-1	1	-

MELEE WEAPONS

WEAPON	RANGE	TYPE	S	AP	D	ABILITIES
Chainaxe	Melee	Melee	+1	-1	1	-
Chainfist	Melee	Melee	x2	-4	2	When attacking with this weapon, you must subtract 1 from the hit roll.
Horrifying mutations	Melee	Melee	User	-2	1	-
Lightning claw	Melee	Melee	User	-2	1	You can re-roll failed wound rolls for this weapon. If a model is armed with two lightning claws, each time it fights it can make 1 additional attack with them.
Power axe	Melee	Melee	+1	-2	1	-
Power maul	Melee	Melee	+2	-1	1	-

KILL TEAM

MODEL	POINTS PER MODEL (Does not include wargear)
Terminator	25
- Terminator Gunner	26
- Terminator Champion	27
Khorne Berzerker	16
- Berzerker Destroyer	17
- Berzerker Champion	17
Possessed	20

RANGED WEAPONS

WEAPON	POINTS PER WEAPON
Boltgun	0
Combi-bolter	4
Combi-flamer	5
Combi-melta	9
Combi-plasma	7
Heavy flamer	5
Plasma pistol	1
Reaper autocannon	5

MELEE WEAPONS

WEAPON	POINTS PER WEAPON
Chainaxe	1
Chainfist	6
Horrifying mutations	0
Lightning claw (single/pair)	1/3
Power axe	2
Power fist	4
Power maul	1
Power sword	1

OTHER WARGEAR

WARGEAR	POINTS PER ITEM
Icon of Wrath	5
Icon of Flame	1
Icon of Despair	3
Icon of Excess	5
Icon of Vengeance	1

DEATH GUARD

Nurgle is the Chaos God of plague and pestilence. His greatest mortal champions are the Death Guard, one of the original Traitor Legions who betrayed the Emperor during the Horus Heresy. Riddled with Nurgle's revolting boons, the Death Guard are amongst the most revolting and resilient warriors in the galaxy.

Where unnatural sicknesses ravage worlds, where filth and foulness sweep away reason, purity and hope, where entropy runs rampant amidst the thunderous drone of a billion daemon-flies, there is the hand of the Death Guard felt. Ten thousand years ago, these warriors were loyal sons of the Emperor. They were renowned for their formidable fortitude and ability to wage war in even the most hazardous conditions. The Death Guard, led by their dour Primarch Mortarion, won countless victories for the Imperium upon worlds saturated with radiation, crawling with alien plagues, or otherwise rendered inimical to human life.

When the Death Guard turned to Chaos, the repulsive blessings of Nurgle only enhanced their already infamous endurance. Their bodies bloated and mutated by daemonic diseases, the Death Guard have become utterly inured to pain. Their rusted armour, leathery flesh and layers of rotting blubber can soak up tremendous punishment, allowing the Death Guard to trudge relentlessly forward and shrug off the worst their enemies can throw at them. In return, the Death Guard wield an array of corroded weapons that they use to bludgeon, hack, dismember, dissolve and lethally infect their victims.

The Lords of Contagion are amongst the greatest of the Death Guard's champions. Clad in hulking Cataphractii armour and blade-horned helms, Lords of Contagion lead their kill teams from the front. They are as aggressive as a rapidly spreading virus, striding unstoppably from one victim to the next with their plaguereaper axes swinging. These baleful figures go about their work with grim efficiency, for the warriors of the Death Guard care nothing for martial flourishes and overt displays of combat prowess.

Blightlord Terminators are amongst the most feared warriors of the 41st Millennium, and make for truly terrifying kill team operatives. Their disease-riddled weapons can reduce even the most resilient foes to bubbling slop in a matter of moments, and those who do not fall to the Terminators' armaments are soon undone by the crawling empyric corruption that pours off them in waves. Enemies fighting back against the arrogant Blightlords find even their greatest efforts coming to naught; between the incredible protective powers of Cataphractii armour and the blessings of Nurgle, these warriors are all but invulnerable.

Deathshroud Terminators are a significantly more sinister battlefield presence. Armed with huge scythes known as manreapers, wreathed in clouds of plague flies and noxious fumes, they advance in virtual silence and hack down any who stand against them with a swift economy of violence. These malevolent warriors are the hand-picked emissaries of Mortarion. They speak with the Daemon Primarch's authority, and enact his judgement upon friend and foe alike. Nothing escapes the notice of the Deathshroud, just as no one escapes their blades once marked for annihilation, no matter how hard they fight or how far they flee.

DEATH GUARD KILL TEAMS

If every model in your kill team has the DEATH GUARD Faction keyword, models in your kill team gain the Inexorable Advance ability, below, and you can use Death Guard Tactics.

Inexorable Advance: Models in your kill team do not suffer the penalty to their hit rolls for shooting Heavy weapons during a battle round in which they moved, or for shooting Assault weapons during a battle round in which they Advanced. In addition, models in your kill team firing Rapid Fire weapons double the number of attacks they make if all of their targets are within 18" (rather than within half the weapon's Range characteristic).

TELEPORT STRIKE

Death Guard Tactic

Use this Tactic at the end of the Movement phase. Choose up to three TERMINATOR models from your kill team that were set up in Reserve and set them up anywhere on the battlefield that is more than 5" away from any enemy models.

1 COMMAND POINT

VETERANS OF THE LONG WAR

Death Guard Tactic

Use this Tactic when a PLAGUE MARINE or TERMINATOR model from your kill team is chosen to attack in the Shooting or Fight phase. You can add 1 to wound rolls for the model's attacks that target IMPERIUM models until the end of the phase.

2 COMMAND POINTS

LORD OF CONTAGION

NAME	M	WS	BS	S	T	W	A	Ld	Sv	Max
Lord of Contagion	4"	2+	2+	4	5	6	4	9	2+	1

This model is armed with a plaguereaper.

WEAPON	RANGE	TYPE	S	AP	D	ABILITIES
Manreaper	Melee	Melee	+3	-3	D3	You can re-roll wound rolls of 1 for this weapon.
Plaguereaper	Melee	Melee	+2	-3	3	You can re-roll wound rolls of 1 for this weapon.

WARGEAR OPTIONS	• This model may replace its plaguereaper with a manreaper.

ABILITIES	**Death to the False Emperor:** If a model with this ability makes an attack in the Fight phase which targets an **IMPERIUM** model, each time you make a hit roll of 6+ you may make an additional attack with the same weapon against the same target. These attacks cannot themselves generate any further attacks. **Disgustingly Resilient:** Each time a model with this ability loses a wound, roll a D6; on a 5+ the model does not lose that wound. **Transhuman Physiology:** Ignore the penalty to this model's hit rolls from one flesh wound it has suffered. **Cataphractii Armour:** This model has a 4+ invulnerable save, but you must halve the result of the dice rolled when determining how far it Advances.
SPECIALISTS	Ferocity, Fortitude, Leadership, Logistics, Melee, Strategist, Strength
FACTION KEYWORD	DEATH GUARD
KEYWORDS	CHAOS, NURGLE, HERETIC ASTARTES, COMMANDER, INFANTRY, TERMINATOR, LORD OF CONTAGION

VECTOR OF CONTAGION

Death Guard Tactic
Lord of Contagion Tactic

Use this Tactic at the start of the battle round if your kill team includes a **LORD OF CONTAGION** that is not shaken. Roll a dice for each enemy model that is within 1" of any model from your kill team that is within 3" of that **LORD OF CONTAGION**; on a 4+ that enemy model suffers a mortal wound.

2 COMMAND POINTS

DEATH GUARD

MODEL	POINTS PER MODEL
Lord of Contagion (Level 1)	114
Lord of Contagion (Level 2)	134
Lord of Contagion (Level 3)	154
Lord of Contagion (Level 4)	179
WARGEAR	**POINTS PER ITEM**
Manreaper	0
Plaguereaper	0

BLIGHTLORD TERMINATOR

NAME	M	WS	BS	S	T	W	A	Ld	Sv	Max
Blightlord Terminator	4"	3+	3+	4	5	2	2	8	2+	-
Blightlord Gunner	4"	3+	3+	4	5	2	2	8	2+	2
Blightlord Fighter	4"	3+	3+	4	5	2	2	8	2+	2
Blightlord Champion	4"	3+	3+	4	5	2	3	9	2+	1

This model is armed with a combi-bolter and either a balesword or a bubotic axe.
Up to two Blightlord Terminators in your kill team can be Blightlord Gunners, up to two Blightlord Terminators in your kill team can be Blightlord Fighters, and one Blightlord Terminator in your kill team can be a Blightlord Champion.

WARGEAR OPTIONS	• This model may replace its combi-bolter with a combi-flamer, combi-melta or combi-plasma. • A Blightlord Gunner may replace their combi-bolter with a plague spewer, reaper autocannon or blight launcher. • A Blightlord Fighter may replace their weapons with a flail of corruption.

ABILITIES

Death to the False Emperor: If a model with this ability makes an attack in the Fight phase which targets an **IMPERIUM** model, each time you make a hit roll of 6+ you may make an additional attack with the same weapon against the same target. These attacks cannot themselves generate any further attacks.

Disgustingly Resilient: Each time a model with this ability loses a wound, roll a D6; on a 5+ the model does not lose that wound.

Transhuman Physiology: Ignore the penalty to this model's hit rolls from one flesh wound it has suffered.

Cataphractii Armour: This model has a 4+ invulnerable save, but you must halve the result of the dice rolled when determining how far it Advances.

Aura of Rust: Each time you make an unmodified wound roll of 6 for one of this model's melee weapons, improve the AP of that attack by 1 (e.g. AP -2 becomes AP -3).

SPECIALISTS	**Leader** (Champion only), **Heavy** (Gunner only), **Combat**, **Demolitions**, **Veteran**, **Zealot**
FACTION KEYWORD	**DEATH GUARD**
KEYWORDS	**CHAOS, NURGLE, HERETIC ASTARTES, INFANTRY, TERMINATOR, BLIGHTLORD TERMINATOR**

DEATHSHROUD TERMINATOR

NAME	M	WS	BS	S	T	W	A	Ld	Sv	Max
Deathshroud Terminator	4"	3+	3+	5	5	2	3	8	2+	-
Deathshroud Champion	4"	3+	3+	5	5	2	4	9	2+	1

This model is armed with a manreaper and plaguespurt gauntlet.
One Deathshroud Terminator in your kill team can be a Deathshroud Champion.

WARGEAR OPTIONS	• A Deathshroud Champion may take a second plaguespurt gauntlet.

ABILITIES	**Death to the False Emperor:** If a model with this ability makes an attack in the Fight phase which targets an IMPERIUM model, each time you make a hit roll of 6+ you may make an additional attack with the same weapon against the same target. These attacks cannot themselves generate any further attacks.	**Transhuman Physiology:** Ignore the penalty to this model's hit rolls from one flesh wound it has suffered.
	Disgustingly Resilient: Each time a model with this ability loses a wound, roll a D6; on a 5+ the model does not lose that wound.	**Cataphractii Armour:** This model has a 4+ invulnerable save, but you must halve the result of the dice rolled when determining how far it Advances.
	Eyes of Mortarion: Add 1 to the Attacks characteristic of COMMANDERS within 3" of any friendly models with this ability.	**Silent Bodyguard:** Roll a D6 each time a COMMANDER is hit by a ranged or melee weapon whilst they are within 3" of any friendly models with this ability. On a 2+ choose one of those models to be hit instead – resolve the remainder of the attack sequence against that model.

SPECIALISTS	Leader (Champion only), **Combat**, **Demolitions**, **Veteran**, **Zealot**

FACTION KEYWORD	DEATH GUARD

KEYWORDS	CHAOS, NURGLE, HERETIC ASTARTES, INFANTRY, TERMINATOR, DEATHSHROUD TERMINATOR

RANGED WEAPONS

WEAPON	RANGE	TYPE	S	AP	D	ABILITIES
Combi-bolter	24"	Rapid Fire 2	4	0	1	-
Combi-flamer	When attacking with this weapon, choose one or both of the profiles below. If you choose both, subtract 1 from all hit rolls made for this weapon.					
- Boltgun	24"	Rapid Fire 1	4	0	1	-
- Flamer	8"	Assault D6	4	0	1	This weapon automatically hits its target.
Combi-melta	When attacking with this weapon, choose one or both of the profiles below. If you choose both, subtract 1 from all hit rolls made for this weapon.					
- Boltgun	24"	Rapid Fire 1	4	0	1	-
- Meltagun	12"	Assault 1	8	-4	D6	If the target is within half range of this weapon, roll two dice when inflicting damage with it and discard the lowest result.
Combi-plasma	When attacking with this weapon, choose one or both of the profiles below. If you choose both, subtract 1 from all hit rolls made for this weapon.					
- Boltgun	24"	Rapid Fire 1	4	0	1	-
- Plasma gun	24"	Rapid Fire 1	7	-3	1	This weapon can be supercharged by the bearer before firing. If they do so, increase the Strength and Damage of the weapon by 1 this turn. On any unmodified hit rolls of 1 when firing supercharge, the bearer is taken out of action after all of the weapon's shots have been resolved.
Plaguespurt gauntlet	6"	Pistol D6	3	0	1	You can re-roll wound rolls of 1 for this weapon. This weapon automatically hits its target.
Reaper autocannon	36"	Heavy 4	7	-1	1	-

MELEE WEAPONS

WEAPON	RANGE	TYPE	S	AP	D	ABILITIES
Balesword	Melee	Melee	User	-3	1	You can re-roll wound rolls of 1 for this weapon.
Manreaper	Melee	Melee	+3	-3	D3	You can re-roll wound rolls of 1 for this weapon.

KILL TEAM

MODEL	POINTS PER MODEL (Does not include wargear)
Blightlord Terminator	40
- Blightlord Gunner	41
- Blightlord Fighter	41
- Blightlord Champion	41
Deathshroud Terminator	50
- Deathshroud Champion	55

MELEE WEAPONS

WEAPON	POINTS PER WEAPON
Balesword	0
Bubotic axe	0
Flail of corruption	0
Manreaper	0

RANGED WEAPONS

WEAPON	POINTS PER WEAPON
Blight launcher	7
Combi-bolter	0
Combi-flamer	1
Combi-melta	5
Combi-plasma	3
Plague spewer	0
Plaguespurt gauntlet (single/pair)	0/3
Reaper autocannon	5

THOUSAND SONS

Once, the Thousand Sons were a loyal Space Marine Legion who fought during the Great Crusade in the service of the Emperor. Yet the Chaos God Tzeentch led their psychically gifted Primarch, Magnus the Red, astray. With his fall, his Legion too was damned, and soon enough a terrible fate overtook the sons of Prospero.

Tzeentch is the Chaos God of change, fate and sorcery. His warping influence spread rapidly through the ranks of the Thousand Sons when they first dedicated themselves to him. With mutation running rife through their Legion, it appeared that the Thousand Sons might be wholly consumed by the unnatural powers they wielded. Instead, the Legion's Chief Librarian, Ahzek Ahriman, performed a mighty spell called the Rubric. Intended to halt the corruption afflicting the Thousand Sons, the spell's effects went much further; it blasted most of the surviving Legionnaires to dust, entombing their residual essence within their sealed suits of power armour for eternity.

Magnus the Red was furious beyond words at what his favoured son had wrought, and exiled Ahriman. Yet it cannot be denied that Ahriman saved the Thousand Sons from rampant change, even if he did so at the cost of their minds and souls.

What remained when the Rubric had done its work were virtual automata. The great majority of the Thousand Sons had become armour-golems animated by ghosts. Only the greatest Sorcerers amongst the XV Legion escaped this fate, and these mighty individuals now took charge of their near-mindless former brethren. The so-called Rubric Marines could still fight, still shoot, and were now immune to doubt, pain or fatigue. They became potent tools of conquest that their sorcerous masters used to further their own twisted agendas.

Now the Thousand Sons operate as interwoven cults and warbands, each following their own fractally elaborate plans for conquest. When such a scheme nears fruition, it is common for a kill team of Scarab Occult Terminators to be deployed to ensure its completion through the application of maximum force. In life, these sublimely skilled and psychically talented warriors once served as the bodyguards of Magnus the Red himself. They engraved arcane formulae and potent spells into their hulking armour, and when the Rubric struck the energies of these cursed inscriptions blended with the remnants of the Terminators' souls. The result was that the Scarab Occult Terminators were wreathed in shimmering shields of sorcerous energy, creating warriors resistant to the perils of empyric transfer, and therefore ideally suited to teleportation assault.

On the attack, these gilded giants hack through their enemies with sweeping blows of their serrated khopeshes, and gun them down with volley after volley of ensorcelled bolts. Meanwhile, the Sorcerer who leads the Rubricae into battle summons the twisting energies of the immaterium with booming words of power. He hurls blasts of mutagenic flame at his enemies, its touch burning them away to multihued embers, transmogrifying them into screaming statues of crystal or warping them into writhing mounds of glistening flesh.

THOUSAND SONS KILL TEAMS

If every model in your kill team has the THOUSAND SONS Faction keyword, models in your kill team gain the Brotherhood of Sorcerers ability below and you can use Thousand Sons Tactics.

Brotherhood of Sorcerers: When it is your turn to choose a PSYKER from your kill team to attempt to manifest psychic powers in this phase, you can choose up to two models from your kill team to do so. Resolve all of one model's attempts before choosing the next model. In addition, the ranges of all psychic powers manifested by models in your kill team are increased by 3".

TELEPORT STRIKE

Thousand Sons Tactic

Use this Tactic at the end of the Movement phase. Choose up to three TERMINATOR models from your kill team that were set up in Reserve and set them up anywhere on the battlefield that is more than 5" away from any enemy models.

1 COMMAND POINT

IMMOVABLE AUTOMATON

Thousand Sons Tactic

Use this Tactic when a Rubric Marine, Rubric Marine Gunner, Scarab Occult Terminator or Scarab Occult Gunner from your kill team is taken out of action. Roll a D6. On a 4+ that model suffers a flesh wound instead.

2 COMMAND POINTS

VETERANS OF THE LONG WAR

Thousand Sons Tactic

Use this Tactic when a RUBRIC MARINE or SCARAB OCCULT TERMINATOR from your kill team is chosen to attack in the Shooting or Fight phase. You can add 1 to wound rolls for the model's attacks that target IMPERIUM models until the end of the phase.

2 COMMAND POINTS

SCARAB OCCULT TERMINATOR

NAME	M	WS	BS	S	T	W	A	Ld	Sv	Max
Scarab Occult Terminator	4"	3+	3+	4	4	2	2	8	2+	-
Scarab Occult Gunner	4"	3+	3+	4	4	2	2	8	2+	2
Scarab Occult Sorcerer	5"	3+	3+	4	4	2	2	9	2+	1

This model is armed with an inferno combi-bolter and power sword.
Up to two Scarab Occult Terminators in your kill team can be Scarab Occult Gunners, and one Scarab Occult Terminator in your kill team can be a Scarab Occult Sorcerer. A Scarab Occult Sorcerer is armed with an inferno combi-bolter and force stave.

WARGEAR OPTIONS	• A Scarab Occult Gunner may replace their inferno combi-bolter with a heavy warpflamer or soulreaper cannon. • Up to two Scarab Occult Terminators or Scarab Occult Gunners in your kill team may take a hellfyre missile rack. • A Scarab Occult Sorcerer may replace their inferno combi-bolter with a power sword.
ABILITIES	**Death to the False Emperor:** If a model with this ability makes an attack in the Fight phase which targets an **IMPERIUM** model, each time you make a hit roll of 6+ you may make an additional attack with the same weapon against the same target. These attacks cannot themselves generate any further attacks. **Transhuman Physiology (Sorcerer only):** Ignore the penalty to this model's hit rolls from one flesh wound it has suffered.	**All is Dust:** Add 1 to saving throws for a Scarab Occult Terminator or Scarab Occult Gunner if the attack has a Damage characteristic of 1. In addition, the -1 modifier to hit rolls for moving and shooting Heavy weapons does not apply to Scarab Occult Gunners. **Terminator Armour:** This model has a 5+ invulnerable save.
PSYKER	A Scarab Occult Sorcerer can attempt to manifest one psychic power and deny one psychic power in each Psychic phase. It knows the *Psybolt* psychic power.
SPECIALISTS	**Leader** (Sorcerer only), **Heavy** (Gunner only), **Combat**, **Demolitions**, **Veteran**
FACTION KEYWORD	THOUSAND SONS
KEYWORDS	CHAOS, TZEENTCH, HERETIC ASTARTES, INFANTRY, PSYKER (Scarab Occult Sorcerer only), TERMINATOR, SCARAB OCCULT TERMINATOR

RANGED WEAPONS

WEAPON	RANGE	TYPE	S	AP	D	ABILITIES
Heavy warpflamer	8"	Heavy D6	5	-2	1	This weapon automatically hits its target.
Hellfyre missile rack	24"	Heavy 2	8	-2	D3	-
Inferno combi-bolter	24"	Rapid Fire 2	4	-2	1	-

MELEE WEAPONS

WEAPON	RANGE	TYPE	S	AP	D	ABILITIES
Power sword	Melee	Melee	User	-3	1	-

KILL TEAM

MODEL	POINTS PER MODEL (Does not include wargear)
Scarab Occult Terminator	32
- Scarab Occult Gunner	33
- Scarab Occult Sorcerer	38

RANGED WEAPONS

WEAPON	POINTS PER WEAPON
Heavy warpflamer	0
Hellfyre missile rack	4
Inferno combi-bolter	0
Soulreaper cannon	3

MELEE WEAPONS

WEAPON	POINTS PER WEAPON
Force stave	0
Power sword	0

ASURYANI

Asuryani warriors fight with flawless poise, singular focus and breathtaking speed and skill. Their technological mastery is so advanced that it appears to the galaxy's other races more akin to sorcery, and their ability to wreak annihilation upon their foes is terrifying to behold.

The Asuryani are the descendants of those Aeldari who fled the Fall aboard immense starships known as craftworlds. So horrified were they by the obsessions and excesses that brought about the cataclysm which shattered their empire, they adopted a rigorous societal model intended to enforce mental and spiritual purity. Such a framework centres around the Paths, hyper-focused disciplines that allow the Asuryani to devote themselves to a single art to the exclusion of all else, honing their minds and souls accordingly. From these Paths do the Aspect Warriors hail.

The Asuryani also took to capturing the souls of their dead within waystones to prevent them from being devoured by Slaanesh. These psychoreactive gems allow the souls to be uploaded to the craftworld's infinity circuit, and there be preserved as ghostly presences. In recent millennia, as the fight for survival has become ever more desperate, the Asuryani have also taken to crafting 'ghost warriors' from wraithbone and investing them with animus through the installation of a spirit stone. These constructs are the product of the Spiritseers' craft, and they are incredibly durable and graceful engines of war. To send the resurrected animus of their ancestors into battle is a dire step indeed, but it is a measure of both the Asuryani's plight and their determination to prevail against all odds.

It is the Aspect Shrines, along with the wraithbone forges of the Spiritseers, that produce many of the Asuryani's most elite warriors. When a kill team must be formed and sent into battle, it is often such lethally skilled operatives that lead the way. In terms of ghost warriors, both Wraithguard and Wraithblades make for exceptionally powerful additions to a kill team. The former erase their enemies from existence with terrifyingly powerful distortion weaponry, while the latter hack their victims apart with semi-sentient swords and axes. The wraithbone bodies of these warriors are phenomenally resilient, while offering the animating spirit almost as much fluidity of movement as they once possessed in life. The ghosts interred within these lithe constructs sometimes require the guidance of the living to realise their full combat potential, however, and it is the gift of the Spiritseers to provide this for them.

Should a mission call for close-combat capability, two types of Aspect Warrior in particular are known for their effectiveness in kill teams. Howling Banshees stun their victims with psionic screams before delivering the killing blow with powered blades that can slice through ceramite. Striking Scorpions, meanwhile, are stealth specialists who slink through the shadows before pouncing upon their victims with chainswords howling and mandiblasters spitting death.

Even the Path of the Outcast – an Aeldari who has fled the asceticism of craftworld life – produces exceptionally skilled warriors, known as Rangers. The greatest of these is Illic Nightspear. Slipping through the enemy lines like a chill breeze, he picks off his victims one at a time with shots so accurate his skill seems supernatural even to his sharp-shooting brothers and sisters.

ASURYANI KILL TEAMS

If every model in your kill team has the ASURYANI Faction keyword, you can use Asuryani Tactics.

MASTERS OF STEALTH

Asuryani Tactic

Use this Tactic at the end of the Movement phase. Choose up to three STRIKING SCORPION models from your kill team that were set up in Reserve and set them up anywhere on the battlefield that is more than 5" away from any enemy models.

1 COMMAND POINT

APPEAR UNBIDDEN

Asuryani Tactic

Use this Tactic at the beginning of the first battle round. Choose up to three RANGER models from your kill team that were set up in Reserve and set them up anywhere on the battlefield that is more than 9" away from any enemy deployment zone.

1 COMMAND POINT

SPIRITSEER

NAME	M	WS	BS	S	T	W	A	Ld	Sv	Max
Spiritseer	7"	2+	2+	3	3	4	2	8	6+	1

This model is armed with a shuriken pistol and witch staff.

WEAPON	RANGE	TYPE	S	AP	D	ABILITIES
Witch staff	Melee	Melee	User	0	2	-

ABILITIES	**Ancient Doom:** You can re-roll failed hit rolls in the Fight phase for this model in a battle round in which it charges or is charged by a SLAANESH model. However, you must add 1 to Nerve tests for this model if it is within 3" of any SLAANESH models. **Battle Focus:** If this model moves or Advances in its Movement phase, weapons (excluding Heavy weapons) are used as if the model had remained stationary. **Rune Armour:** This model has a 4+ invulnerable save.
PSYKER	This model can attempt to manifest one psychic power and deny one psychic power in each Psychic phase. It knows the *Psybolt* psychic power as well as one psychic power generated from the Runes of Battle discipline (see *Kill Team: Commanders*).
SPECIALISTS	Leadership, Melee, Psyker, Stealth, Strategist
FACTION KEYWORD	ASURYANI
KEYWORDS	AELDARI, SPIRIT HOST, COMMANDER, INFANTRY, PSYKER, SPIRITSEER

SPIRIT MARK

Asuryani Tactic
Spiritseer Aura Tactic

Use this Tactic at the start of the battle round if your kill team includes a SPIRITSEER. That model gains the following aura ability until the end of the battle round:

As long as this model is not shaken, you can re-roll hit rolls of 1 for friendly SPIRIT HOST models that target enemy models within 6" of this model.

1 COMMAND POINT

ASURYANI	
MODEL	**POINTS PER MODEL**
Spiritseer (Level 1)	61
Spiritseer (Level 2)	76
Spiritseer (Level 3)	91
Spiritseer (Level 4)	116
WARGEAR	**POINTS PER ITEM**
Shuriken pistol	0
Witch staff	0

ILLIC NIGHTSPEAR

NAME	M	WS	BS	S	T	W	A	Ld	Sv	Max
Illic Nightspear	7"	2+	2+	3	3	5	4	9	5+	1

This model is armed with Voidbringer, a shuriken pistol and a power sword.
Only one of this model may be included on your command roster.

WEAPON	RANGE	TYPE	S	AP	D	ABILITIES
Voidbringer	48"	Heavy 1	4	-3	3	A model firing this weapon does not suffer the penalty to hit rolls for the target being at long range. This weapon wounds on a 2+. Each time you roll a wound roll of 6+ for this weapon, it inflicts a mortal wound in addition to any other damage.

ABILITIES	
	Ancient Doom: You can re-roll failed hit rolls in the Fight phase for this model in a battle round in which it charges or is charged by a SLAANESH model. However, you must add 1 to Nerve tests for this model if it is within 3" of any SLAANESH models.
	Battle Focus: If this model moves or Advances in its Movement phase, weapons (excluding Heavy weapons) are used as if the model had remained stationary.
	Hunter Unseen: If this model is obscured when it is the target of a shooting attack, improve its Save characteristic to 3+ until that attack has been resolved.
	Bringer of the True Death: You can re-roll hit and wound rolls of 1 for this model's attacks that target NECRONS models.

SPECIALISTS	Legendary Hunter (Level 3)
FACTION KEYWORD	ASURYANI
KEYWORDS	AELDARI, WARHOST, ALAITOC, COMMANDER, INFANTRY, RANGER, ILLIC NIGHTSPEAR

WAYFORGER

Asuryani Tactic
Illic Nightspear Tactic

Use this Tactic at the start of the Shooting phase if your kill team includes Illic Nightspear and that model is not shaken. That model becomes Readied, and for the purposes of making shooting attacks in this phase, that model is considered to have remained stationary in the preceding Move phase.

2 COMMAND POINTS

ASURYANI	
MODEL	**POINTS PER MODEL**
Illic Nightspear (Level 3)	79
WARGEAR	**POINTS PER ITEM**
Power sword	0
Shuriken pistol	0
Voidbringer	0

WRAITHGUARD

NAME	M	WS	BS	S	T	W	A	Ld	Sv	Max
Wraithguard	5"	3+	3+	5	6	3	1	9	3+	-

This model is armed with a wraithcannon and Wraithguard fists

WARGEAR OPTIONS
- This model may replace its wraithcannon with a D-scythe.

ABILITIES

Ancient Doom: You can re-roll failed hit rolls in the Fight phase for this model in a battle round in which it charges or is charged by a **SLAANESH** model. However, you must add 1 to Nerve tests for this model if it is within 3" of any **SLAANESH** models.

Implacable: This model can shoot or React even if it Fell Back or Retreated earlier in the battle round.

Ghost Warrior: This model cannot gain experience.

SPECIALISTS Demolitions, Heavy, Veteran

FACTION KEYWORD ASURYANI

KEYWORDS AELDARI, SPIRIT HOST, INFANTRY, WRAITH CONSTRUCT, WRAITHGUARD

WRAITHBLADE

NAME	M	WS	BS	S	T	W	A	Ld	Sv	Max
Wraithblade	5"	3+	3+	5	6	3	2	9	3+	-

This model is armed with ghostswords.

WARGEAR OPTIONS
- This model may replace its ghostswords with a ghostaxe and forceshield.

ABILITIES

Ancient Doom: You can re-roll failed hit rolls in the Fight phase for this model in a battle round in which it charges or is charged by a **SLAANESH** model. However, you must add 1 to Nerve tests for this model if it is within 3" of any **SLAANESH** models.

Fires of Wrath: Add 1 to the Attacks characteristic of this model in a battle round in which it charged.

Forceshield: A model with a forceshield has a 4+ invulnerable save.

Ghost Warrior: This model cannot gain experience.

SPECIALISTS Combat, Veteran, Zealot

FACTION KEYWORD ASURYANI

KEYWORDS AELDARI, SPIRIT HOST, INFANTRY, WRAITH CONSTRUCT, WRAITHBLADE

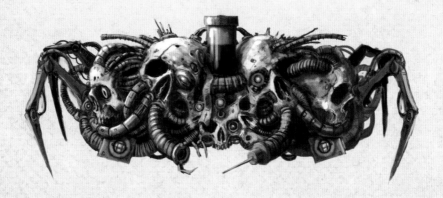

STRIKING SCORPION

NAME	M	WS	BS	S	T	W	A	Ld	Sv	Max
Striking Scorpion	7"	3+	3+	3	3	1	2	8	3+	-
Striking Scorpion Exarch	7"	3+	3+	3	3	2	3	8	3+	1

This model is armed with a shuriken pistol, a scorpion chainsword and plasma grenades.
One Striking Scorpion in your kill team can be a Striking Scorpion Exarch.

WARGEAR OPTIONS	• A Striking Scorpion Exarch may replace their shuriken pistol with a scorpion's claw.
	• A Striking Scorpion Exarch may replace their scorpion chainsword with a biting blade.

ABILITIES	**Ancient Doom:** You can re-roll failed hit rolls in the Fight phase for this model in a battle round in which it charges or is charged by a **Slaanesh** model. However, you must add 1 to Nerve tests for this model if it is within 3" of any **Slaanesh** models.	**Mandiblasters:** At the beginning of the Fight phase, you can pick a single enemy model within 1" of this model. Roll a D6; on a roll of 6, the enemy model suffers a mortal wound.
	Battle Focus: If this model moves or Advances in its Movement phase, weapons (excluding Heavy weapons) are used as if the model had remained stationary.	**Sustained Attack:** Each time you roll an unmodified hit roll of 6 when making a close combat attack for a Striking Scorpion Exarch, that model can immediately make another close combat attack using the same weapon against the same target. These extra attacks cannot generate any additional attacks.
	Shadow Strike: Add 1 to hit rolls for attacks made by this model that target a model that is obscured or when there is intervening terrain.	

SPECIALISTS	**Leader** (Exarch only), **Combat, Demolitions, Scout, Stealth, Veteran, Zealot**
FACTION KEYWORD	**Asuryani**
KEYWORDS	**Aeldari, Aspect Warrior, Infantry, Striking Scorpion**

HOWLING BANSHEE

NAME	M	WS	BS	S	T	W	A	Ld	Sv	Max
Howling Banshee	8"	3+	3+	3	3	1	2	8	4+	-
Howling Banshee Exarch	8"	3+	3+	3	3	2	3	8	4+	1

This model is armed with a with a shuriken pistol and power sword.
One Howling Banshee in your kill team can be a Howling Banshee Exarch.

WARGEAR OPTIONS	• A Howling Banshee Exarch may replace their power sword with an executioner.
	• A Howling Banshee Exarch may replace their shuriken pistol and power sword with mirrorswords.

ABILITIES	**Ancient Doom:** You can re-roll failed hit rolls in the Fight phase for this model in a battle round in which it charges or is charged by a **Slaanesh** model. However, you must add 1 to Nerve tests for this model if it is within 3" of any **Slaanesh** models.	**Acrobatic:** You can re-roll failed charge rolls for this model.
		Banshee Mask: Enemy models cannot React when they are a target of this model's charge.
	Battle Focus: If this model moves or Advances in its Movement phase, weapons (excluding Heavy weapons) are used as if the model had remained stationary.	**War Shout:** Your opponents must subtract 1 from hit rolls in the Fight phase for attacks that target a Howling Banshee Exarch.

SPECIALISTS	**Leader** (Exarch only), **Combat, Comms, Veteran, Zealot**
FACTION KEYWORD	**Asuryani**
KEYWORDS	**Aeldari, Aspect Warrior, Infantry, Howling Banshee**

RANGED WEAPONS

WEAPON	RANGE	TYPE	S	AP	D	ABILITIES
D-scythe	8"	Assault D3	10	-4	1	This weapon automatically hits its target.
Scorpion's claw	This weapon can be used as a ranged weapon and a melee weapon. When making shooting attacks or firing Overwatch with this weapon, use the ranged profile; when making close combat attacks, use the melee profile.					
- Ranged	12"	Assault 2	4	0	1	Each time you make a wound roll of 6+ for this weapon, that hit is resolved with an AP of -3.
- Melee	Melee	Melee	x2	-3	D3	-
Wraithcannon	12"	Assault 1	10	-4	D6	-

MELEE WEAPONS

WEAPON	RANGE	TYPE	S	AP	D	ABILITIES
Biting blade	Melee	Melee	+2	-1	2	-
Executioner	Melee	Melee	+1	-3	D3	-
Ghostaxe	Melee	Melee	+2	-3	D3	When attacking with this weapon, you must subtract 1 from the hit roll.
Ghostswords	Melee	Melee	+1	-3	1	Each time the bearer fights, it can make 1 additional attack with this weapon.
Power sword	Melee	Melee	User	-3	1	-
Mirrorswords	Melee	Melee	User	-2	1	You can re-roll failed hit rolls when attacking with this weapon.
Scorpion chainsword	Melee	Melee	+1	0	1	-
Wraithguard fists	Melee	Melee	User	-1	D3	-

KILL TEAM

MODEL	POINTS PER MODEL (Does not include wargear)
Howling Banshee	11
- Howling Banshee Exarch	14
Striking Scorpion	12
- Striking Scorpion Exarch	14
Wraithblade	36
Wraithguard	41

OTHER WARGEAR

WARGEAR	POINTS PER ITEM
Forceshield	8

RANGED WEAPONS

WEAPON	POINTS PER WEAPON
D-scythe	0
Plasma grenades	0
Scorpion's claw	7
Shuriken pistol	0
Wraithcannon	0

MELEE WEAPONS

WEAPON	POINTS PER WEAPON
Biting blade	3
Executioner	3
Ghostaxe	1
Ghostswords	0
Power sword	0
Mirrorswords	0
Scorpion chainsword	0
Wraithguard fists	0

DRUKHARI

Hailing from the dark city of Commorragh, the Drukhari are the twisted descendants of the ancient Aeldari whose decadence and cruelty brought about the Fall. These eldritch xenos radiate unrepentant wickedness and towering arrogance, and see all other races in the galaxy as nothing more than livestock to be exploited at will.

In a grim and terrible age where merciless savagery is the norm, still the Drukhari are remarkable for their sadism. They are creatures of nightmare, beings of vast intellect and arcane technology who feed off the terror and agony of their victims. The Drukhari are vampires of suffering, whose entire existence revolves around inflicting the most extreme horrors upon their enemies in order to sustain their own withering souls. Both darkly beautiful and ghastly beyond words, the Drukhari emerge from the shadows in swift-striking raiding parties. They leave a trail of butchery and visceral horror in their wake before snatching up the choicest slaves and vanishing back to Commorragh to begin their revels anew.

Some raids are particularly vital; perhaps a great hero or spiritual leader must be stolen away in order to spread panic through a world's populace, a shield generator must be brought down before the main assault begins, or a hallucinogenic plague must be unleashed. Whatever the case, such crucial strikes are often entrusted to the most skilful, most monstrous or strangest of the Drukhari.

When the tightest defences must be penetrated, the shadowy Mandrakes of Aelindrach are the secret weapon of many a Drukhari Archon. Malefic inhabitants of a shattered nether-realm, these appalling creatures can emerge from pools of shadow at will, creep through reflective surfaces and slither from hairline cracks in reality itself to attack even the most secure positions. Hurling blasts of freezing balefire, dragging their ragged knives across throats and plucking out eyes, the Mandrakes bring with them a pall of unnatural cold and send chilling whispers echoing through the enemy stronghold. Soon, the only living foes that remain are gibbering madmen hunched in corners, awaiting their inevitable doom.

Far less subtle but every bit as terrifying are the monstrous servants of the Haemonculus Covens. Wracks are flesh-stitched torturers who bring vile weapons and foul bladed deformities to bear against their foes. Grotesques, meanwhile, are slave warriors that are bulked up into berserk killers with macro-steroids and other vile alchemical agents, these hulking monsters feel neither pain nor fear. They smash into their victims with the fury of the damned, for they truly have nothing left to lose, and their masters delight in unleashing them upon key enemy targets and watching as hideous carnage unfolds.

Most sublimely skilled in close combat of all the Drukhari are the Incubi. Fighting in mercenary bands for the highest bidder, these faceless killers are the dark mirror of Asuryani Aspect Warriors, and train in their bloody profession obsessively. With their vicious klaives splitting the air, the Incubi mercilessly carve a red path through all who stand in their way, completing their assigned mission with vicious efficiency before vanishing as swiftly as they appeared.

DRUKHARI KILL TEAMS

If every model in your kill team has the DRUKHARI Faction keyword, you can use Drukhari Tactics.

FROM OUT OF THE SHADOWS

Drukhari Tactic

Use this Tactic at the end of the Movement phase. Choose up to three MANDRAKE models from your kill team that were set up in Reserve and set them up anywhere on the battlefield that is more than 5" away from any enemy models.

1 COMMAND POINT

WRACK

NAME	M	WS	BS	S	T	W	A	Ld	Sv	Max
Wrack	8"	3+	3+	4	3	1	3	7	7+	-
Wrack Gunner	8"	3+	3+	4	3	1	3	7	7+	2
Acothyst	8"	3+	3+	4	3	1	4	8	7+	1

This model is armed with Haemonculus tools.
Up to two Wracks in your kill team can be Wrack Gunners, and one Wrack in your kill team can be an Acothyst.

WARGEAR OPTIONS	• A Wrack Gunner may take a liquifier gun or ossefactor. • An Acothyst may take a hexrifle, liquifier gun or stinger pistol. • An Acothyst may replace its Haemonculus tools with an agoniser, electrocorrosive whip, flesh gauntlet, mindphase gauntlet, scissorhand or venom blade.
ABILITIES	**Power From Pain** (see the *Kill Team Core Manual*) **Insensible to Pain:** This model has a 5+ invulnerable save.
SPECIALISTS	**Leader** (Acothyst only), **Heavy** (Gunner only), **Combat**, **Demolitions**, **Medic**, **Veteran**, **Zealot**
FACTION KEYWORD	DRUKHARI
KEYWORDS	AELDARI, HAEMONCULUS COVEN, INFANTRY, WRACK

INCUBUS

NAME	M	WS	BS	S	T	W	A	Ld	Sv	Max
Incubus	7"	3+	3+	3	3	1	3	8	3+	-
Klaivex	7"	3+	3+	3	3	2	4	9	3+	1

This model is armed with a klaive.
One Incubus in your kill team can be a Klaivex.

ABILITIES	**Power From Pain** (see the *Kill Team Core Manual*)
	Tormentors: Your opponents must add 1 to Nerve tests taken for models that are within 3" of any enemy models with this ability.
	Lethal Precision: Add 2 to the Damage characteristic of a close combat attack made by a Klaivex if the wound roll for the attack is 6+.
SPECIALISTS	**Leader** (Klaivex only), **Combat**, **Veteran**, **Zealot**
FACTION KEYWORD	**Drukhari**
KEYWORDS	**Aeldari, Infantry, Incubus**

GROTESQUE

NAME	M	WS	BS	S	T	W	A	Ld	Sv	Max
Grotesque	7"	3+	6+	5	5	4	4	8	6+	-

This model is armed with a monstrous cleaver and flesh gauntlet.

WARGEAR OPTIONS	• This model may replace its monstrous cleaver with a liquifier gun.	
ABILITIES	**Power From Pain** (see the *Kill Team Core Manual*)	**Insensible to Pain:** This model has a 5+ invulnerable save.
SPECIALISTS	**Combat**, **Demolitions**, **Zealot**	
FACTION KEYWORD	**Drukhari**	
KEYWORDS	**Aeldari, Haemonculus Coven, Infantry, Grotesque**	

MANDRAKE

NAME	M	WS	BS	S	T	W	A	Ld	Sv	Max
Mandrake	8"	3+	3+	4	3	1	3	7	7+	-
Nightfiend	8"	3+	3+	4	3	1	4	8	7+	1

This model is armed with a glimmersteel blade and baleblast.

WARGEAR OPTIONS	• One Mandrake in your kill team can be a Nightfiend.
ABILITIES	**Power From Pain** (see the *Kill Team Core Manual*) **Shrouded From Sight:** Subtract 1 from the hit rolls for attacks that target this model. In addition, this model has a 5+ invulnerable save.
SPECIALISTS	**Leader** (Nightfiend only), **Combat**, **Scout**, **Veteran**, **Zealot**
FACTION KEYWORD	**Drukhari**
KEYWORDS	**Aeldari, Infantry, Mandrake**

RANGED WEAPONS

WEAPON	RANGE	TYPE	S	AP	D	ABILITIES
Baleblast	18"	Assault 2	4	-1	1	Each time you make a wound roll of 6+ for this weapon, the target suffers a mortal wound in addition to any other damage.
Hexrifle	36"	Heavy 1	4	-1	1	A model firing a hexrifle does not suffer the penalty to hit rolls for the target being at long range. Each time you roll a wound roll of 6+ for this weapon, it inflicts a mortal wound in addition to any other damage.
Liquifier gun	8"	Assault D6	3	-D3	1	Each time this weapon is fired, roll a D3 to determine its AP for those attacks. For example, if you rolled a 1, this weapon would have an AP of -1. This weapon automatically hits its target.
Ossefactor	24"	Assault 1	*	-3	1	This weapon always wounds on a roll of 2+. If a model is taken out of action by an attack made by this weapon, roll a D6 for each model within 2" of that model. On a roll of 5+ that model suffers a mortal wound.
Stinger pistol	12"	Pistol 1	*	0	1	This weapon always wounds on a roll of 2+.

MELEE WEAPONS

WEAPON	RANGE	TYPE	S	AP	D	ABILITIES
Electrocorrosive whip	Melee	Melee	*	-2	2	This weapon always wounds on a roll of 4+.
Flesh gauntlet	Melee	Melee	User	0	1	Each time you roll a wound roll of 6+ for this weapon the target suffers a mortal wound in addition to any other damage.
Glimmersteel blade	Melee	Melee	User	-1	1	-
Haemonculus tools	Melee	Melee	*	0	1	This weapon always wounds on a roll of 4+.
Klaive	Melee	Melee	+1	-3	1	-
Mindphase gauntlet	Melee	Melee	User	0	2	-
Monstrous cleaver	Melee	Melee	User	-2	1	Each time the bearer fights, it can make 1 additional attack with this weapon.
Scissorhand	Melee	Melee	*	-1	1	Each time the bearer fights, it can make 1 additional attack with this weapon. This weapon always wounds on a roll of 4+.
Venom blade	Melee	Melee	*	0	1	This weapon always wounds on a roll of 2+.

KILL TEAM

MODEL	POINTS PER MODEL (Does not include wargear)
Grotesque	38
Incubus	13
- Klaivex	16
Mandrake	12
- Nightfiend	13
Wrack	8
- Wrack Gunner	9
- Acothyst	9

MELEE WEAPONS

WEAPON	POINTS PER WEAPON
Agoniser	1
Electrocorrosive whip	3
Flesh gauntlet	0
Glimmersteel blade	0
Haemonculus tools	0
Klaive	0
Mindphase gauntlet	1
Monstrous cleaver	0
Scissorhand	2
Venom blade	1

RANGED WEAPONS

WEAPON	POINTS PER WEAPON
Baleblast	0
Hexrifle	1
Liquifier gun	4
Ossefactor	5
Stinger pistol	1

NECRONS

The Necrons are a race of ancient android warriors. Millions of years ago they descended into stasis crypts to slumber through the aeons, and now they are waking to find the galaxy much changed. Determined to reclaim their empire of old, the Necrons purge all other sentient beings from the stars without mercy.

The Necrons are a fearsome and unnatural form of life. Many thousands of years ago they exchanged ephemeral bodies of flesh and blood for shells of living metal. As well as enduring the slow grind of centuries, the Necrons are capable of shrugging off incredible amounts of damage. They ignore plagues and parasites that would spell death for organic creatures, and can stride unharmed through raging fires, lethal sub-zero temperatures and airless vacuums. Even should a Necron fall in battle, their ruined bodies simply teleport away in a flare of emerald light, returned by reanimation protocols to their stasis crypts where they undergo repairs before marching out to war once again.

The price of this virtual immortality is steep, however. Many lower orders of Necrons lost all but their most basic sentience during the process of biotransference, and even the higher-ranking warriors are enslaved to the will of their lords. Only the Necron nobility possess true autonomy, and each of these beings pursues their own agendas with single-minded determination. They issue their edicts to mighty servant-warriors who march out to see their wills done.

Such is the lot of the Lychguard. Trusted lieutenants and dedicated bodyguards, these towering warriors inhabit some of the most powerful bodies gifted to any Necron soldier. Their mental architecture is elaborate enough to permit a degree of operational independence, and even allows for speech and hyper-logical reasoning within certain parameters. The one real limitation of Lychguard is an absolute loyalty to the Lords or phaerons they serve, a programmed adoration for their rulers that sees the Lychguard stride gladly into the heaviest fire and the greatest dangers in order to protect their master and see his enemies laid low.

The martial might of the Lychguard is indisputable. Their armoured bodies are all but impervious to small arms fire, and their hyperphase swords and war scythes make short work of even the most formidable foes. Lychguard are exceptionally powerful kill team operatives, for a mere handful of these warriors can tirelessly hack through tides of enemies in order to complete a mission.

Triarch Praetorians, conversely, are amongst those few Necrons not bound to the will of an Overlord. Instead, this judicial order of warriors stands aloof, their mission to police and enforce the codes of conduct set down by the ancient Triarch that once ruled the Necrons. To the Praetorians, the concept of honour is all. They will as swiftly raise their rods of covenant and particle casters against a Necron ruler who breaks the code as they will against those younger races who have intruded upon the Necrons' ancient holdings and now – in their ignorance – have the temerity to claim them as their own.

Triarch Praetorians set their own goals and missions, and possess their own cunning means of seeing them completed. Not least amongst these is their ability to hover over the battlefield using their gravity-repelling harnesses to strike deep behind enemy lines where they can land the most decisive blow.

NECRON KILL TEAMS

If every model in your kill team has the NECRONS Faction keyword, you can use Necrons Tactics.

HUNTERS FROM HYPERSPACE

Necrons Tactic

Use this Tactic at the end of the Movement phase. Choose up to three DEATHMARK models from your kill team that were set up in Reserve and set them up anywhere on the battlefield that is more than 5" away from any enemy models.

1 COMMAND POINT

RESURRECTION PROTOCOLS

Necrons Tactic

Use this Tactic when your Leader is slain. Instead of removing the model, place it on its side. At the end of the phase, roll a D6. On a 4+ the model is no longer slain: stand the model up again as close as possible to its previous position, but more than 1" away from enemy models, with 1 wound remaining and no flesh wounds. If a model is still on the battlefield at the end of the battle after having been resurrected in this way, it is not considered to have been taken out of action for victory points purposes. You can only use this Tactic once per battle.

2 COMMAND POINTS

TIRELESS ADVANCE

Necrons Tactic

Use this Tactic at the start of the Shooting phase. One model of your choice from your kill team becomes Readied (even if it moved in the previous Movement phase) and may shoot in this phase as if they had not moved in the Movement phase. This Tactic may not be used on a model that is within 1" of an enemy model.

1 COMMAND POINT

HAUNTING HORRORS

Necrons Tactic

Use this Tactic at the end of the Movement phase. Choose up to three FLAYED ONE models from your kill team that were set up in Reserve and set them up anywhere on the battlefield that is more than 5" away from any enemy models.

1 COMMAND POINT

ENTROPIC STRIKE

Necrons Tactic

Use this Tactic when you choose a model in your kill team to fight in the Fight phase. Until the end of the phase, if that model's attacks reduce a target to 0 wounds, add 1 to the Injury roll you make for the target.

1 COMMAND POINT

ASSURED DISINTEGRATION

Necrons Tactic

Use this Tactic when you choose a DEATHMARK from your kill team to shoot in the Shooting phase. Until the end of the phase you may re-roll hit rolls made for that model.

1 COMMAND POINT

DEATHLESS IRE

Necrons Tactic

Use this Tactic when a model from your kill team suffers a flesh wound as the result of an Injury roll. It is shaken instead.

2 COMMAND POINTS

LYCHGUARD

NAME	M	WS	BS	S	T	W	A	Ld	Sv	Max
Lychguard	5"	3+	3+	5	5	2	2	10	3+	-

This model is armed with a warscythe.

WARGEAR OPTIONS	• This model may replace its warscythe with a hyperphase sword and dispersion shield.
ABILITIES	**Reanimation Protocols:** When an Injury roll is made for this model, on an unmodified roll of 6 the model is not taken out of action and does not suffer a flesh wound. Instead it is restored to 1 wound remaining with no flesh wounds. **Dispersion Shield:** A model with a dispersion shield has a 4+ invulnerable save.	**Guardian Protocols:** Roll a D6 each time a **COMMANDER** loses a wound whilst they are within 3" of any friendly models with this ability; on a 2+ choose one of those models to intercept that hit – the **COMMANDER** does not lose a wound but the model you chose suffers a mortal wound.
SPECIALISTS	**Leader, Combat, Comms, Veteran, Zealot**
FACTION KEYWORD	**NECRONS**
KEYWORDS	**INFANTRY, LYCHGUARD**

TRIARCH PRAETORIAN

NAME	M	WS	BS	S	T	W	A	Ld	Sv	Max
Triarch Praetorian	10"	3+	3+	5	5	2	2	10	3+	-

This model is armed with a rod of covenant.

WARGEAR OPTIONS	• This model may replace its rod of covenant with a voidblade and particle caster.
ABILITIES	**Reanimation Protocols:** When an Injury roll is made for this model, on an unmodified roll of 6 the model is not taken out of action and does not suffer a flesh wound. Instead it is restored to 1 wound remaining with no flesh wounds.	**A Purpose Unshakeable:** This model automatically passes Nerve tests.
SPECIALISTS	**Leader, Combat, Comms, Veteran, Zealot**
FACTION KEYWORD	**NECRONS**
KEYWORDS	**INFANTRY, FLY, TRIARCH PRAETORIAN**

RANGED WEAPONS

WEAPON	RANGE	TYPE	S	AP	D	ABILITIES
Particle caster	12"	Pistol 1	6	0	1	-
Rod of covenant	This weapon can be used as a ranged weapon and a melee weapon. When making shooting attacks or firing Overwatch with this weapon, use the ranged profile; when making close combat attacks, use the melee profile.					
- Ranged	12"	Assault 1	5	-3	1	-
- Melee	Melee	Melee	User	-3	1	-

MELEE WEAPONS

WEAPON	RANGE	TYPE	S	AP	D	ABILITIES
Hyperphase sword	Melee	Melee	+1	-3	1	-
Voidblade	Melee	Melee	User	-3	1	Each time the bearer fights, it can make 1 additional attack with this weapon.
Warscythe	Melee	Melee	+2	-4	2	-

KILL TEAM

MODEL	POINTS PER MODEL (Does not include wargear)
Lychguard	20
Triarch Praetorian	26

RANGED WEAPONS

WEAPON	POINTS PER WEAPON
Particle caster	0
Rod of covenant	0

OTHER WARGEAR

WARGEAR	POINTS PER ITEM
Dispersion shield	5

MELEE WEAPONS

WEAPON	POINTS PER WEAPON
Hyperphase sword	0
Voidblade	1
Warscythe	0

ORKS

The Orks are an incredibly warlike and numerous race. They infest the galaxy from end to end, rampaging through the void in fleets of ramshackle warships and falling upon every planet whose defenders may be able to offer them a decent fight. Orks live for battle, this being the main area in which these brutish xenos excel.

Orks are big, green and mean. They are walking mounds of muscle and belligerence, so tough that they can fight on through wounds that would see a human dead three times over, and so strong that they can batter their way through a bulkhead door given the chance. Ork technology is as crude and robust as the warriors that wield it. It is all heavy iron plates and spiky bits, with its workings cobbled together from scrap but no less effective for it. The greenskin hordes defeat their enemies through brute force, bloody-minded savagery and sheer weight of numbers, elementary tactics that have seen the Orks conquer vast swathes of the galaxy time and again.

Might makes right in Ork society. The largest and most ferocious warriors accrue the best loot and the most authority. So it is that the greenskin equivalent of elite kill team operatives are typically just the largest Orks in a warband, toting the biggest shootas and choppas and clad in the heaviest armour they can get their hands on.

Nobz and Meganobz make up the bulk of elite Ork kill teams. These brutes are one rung below their tribe's Warboss in terms of societal standing, and they delight in throwing their weight around. Nobz go to battle clad in 'eavy armour and brandishing massive guns, powered crushing klaws and revving, chain-bladed choppas. Meganobz are more fearsome still, for they wear motor-driven suits of mega armour – the closest equivalent the Orks have to the Terminator armour of the Space Marines. While far less advanced, mega armour can still soak up a direct hit from an artillery shell, and the array of devastating weaponry the Meganobz wield with their piston-enhanced might can reduce even the mightiest enemy warriors to ruin.

Other kill teams may be comprised of Flash Gitz. These swaggering mercenaries travel the space lanes in smoke-belching kroozers and hire their services out to whatever Warboss has the teef to pay their exorbitant fees. The price is worth paying, for Flash Gitz wield snazzguns, hefty weapons that can – with a single pull of the trigger – unleash deafening salvoes of rockets, bullets and energy blasts capable of chewing through rank upon rank of the foe.

As well as mobs of hulking bully boys, the list of elite Ork operatives includes occasional warriors who exemplify the more cunning side of greenskin nature. Perhaps the most famous of these is Boss Snikrot, the Blood Axe Kommando boss who has haunted the equatorial jungles of Armageddon for many years. Snikrot is as devious and savage as they come, leading his ladz in daring night-raids and vicious ambushes that see the surrounding jungle turn red with blood. Snikrot revels in leaving his enemies' heads on spikes as a warning to all, for he understands well the value of an enemy's terror.

ORK KILL TEAMS

If every model in your kill team has the ORKS Faction keyword, you can use Orks Tactics.

KUNNIN' INFILTRATORS

Orks Tactic

Use this Tactic at the end of the Movement phase. Choose up to three KOMMANDO models from your kill team that were set up in Reserve and set them up anywhere on the battlefield that is more than 5" away from any enemy models.

1 COMMAND POINT

DEAD 'ARD

Orks Tactic

Use this Tactic when a model from your kill team suffers a mortal wound. Roll a D6 for that mortal wound, and each other mortal wound suffered by that model for the rest of the phase: on a 5+ the mortal wound is ignored and has no effect.

1 COMMAND POINT

INDISCRIMINATE DAKKA

Orks Tactic

Use this Tactic after firing Overwatch with one of your models. You can immediately fire Overwatch again.

1 COMMAND POINT

PYROMANIAK

Orks Tactic

Use this Tactic when you choose for a model to shoot with a burna. The burna makes D6 attacks instead of D3 this phase.

1 COMMAND POINT

ITCHIN' FOR A FIGHT!

Orks Tactic

Use this Tactic when you choose a model in your kill team to fight in the Fight phase. You can make one additional attack with that model for each enemy model within 1" of it.

2 COMMAND POINTS

'ERE WE GO, 'ERE WE GO!

Orks Tactic

Use this Tactic after making a charge roll for one of your models. Re-roll one of the dice.

1 COMMAND POINT

WAAAGH!

Orks Tactic

Use this Tactic when it is your turn to move in the Movement phase and your Leader is on the battlefield and not shaken. For the duration of that phase, add 1" to the Move characteristic of all models in your kill team, and add 1 to their Advance and charge rolls.

2 COMMAND POINTS

NOB

NAME	M	WS	BS	S	T	W	A	Ld	Sv	Max
Nob	5"	3+	5+	5	4	2	3	6	4+	-
Boss Nob	5"	3+	5+	5	4	2	3	7	4+	1
Ammo Runt	5"	5+	4+	3	3	1	1	4	6+	2

This model is armed with a slugga, choppa and stikkbombs.
One Nob in your kill team can be a Boss Nob, and up to two Nobz in your kill team can instead be Ammo Runts. An Ammo Runt is armed with stikkbombs.

WARGEAR OPTIONS	• A Nob or Boss Nob may replace its slugga and choppa with up to two different weapons from the following list: big choppa, choppa, killsaw, power klaw, power stabba or slugga. • A Nob or Boss Nob may also be armed with a kombi-weapon with rokkit launcha or kombi-weapon with skorcha. • Up to two Nobz or up to one Nob and a Boss Nob in your kill team may have cybork bodies.
ABILITIES	**'Ere We Go:** Re-roll failed charge rolls for this model. **Keepin' Order:** When you make an unmodified roll of 6 for a Nerve test taken for a model within 3" of a friendly model with this ability, that Nerve test is passed. **Cybork Body:** Each time a model with a Cybork body loses a wound, roll a D6; on a 6 that wound is not lost. **Ammo Runt:** Ammo Runts cannot be specialists. Each Ammo Runt (if they are not shaken) can supply one friendly model within 2" with ammo once per Shooting phase. When they do so, you can re-roll one hit roll for a shooting attack made by that model.
SPECIALISTS	**Leader** (Boss Nob only), **Combat, Comms, Demolitions, Veteran**
FACTION KEYWORD	**ORKS**
KEYWORDS	**INFANTRY, NOB** (Ammo Runt is **INFANTRY, GRETCHIN**)

MEGANOB

NAME	M	WS	BS	S	T	W	A	Ld	Sv	Max
Meganob	4"	3+	5+	5	4	3	3	6	2+	-
Boss Meganob	4"	3+	5+	5	4	3	3	7	2+	1

This model is armed with a kustom shoota, power klaw and stikkbombs. One Meganob in your kill team can be a Boss Meganob.

WARGEAR OPTIONS	• This model may replace its kustom shoota and power klaw with two killsaws. • This model may replace its kustom shoota with a kombi-weapon with skorcha or kombi-weapon with rokkit launcha.
ABILITIES	**'Ere We Go:** Re-roll failed charge rolls for this model. **Keepin' Order:** When you make an unmodified roll of 6 for a Nerve test taken for a model within 3" of a friendly model with this ability, that Nerve test is passed.
SPECIALISTS	**Leader** (Boss Meganob only), **Combat, Comms, Demolitions, Veteran**
FACTION KEYWORD	**ORKS**
KEYWORDS	**INFANTRY, MEGA ARMOUR, NOB, MEGANOB**

FLASH GIT

NAME	M	WS	BS	S	T	W	A	Ld	Sv	Max
Flash Git	5"	3+	4+	5	4	2	3	6	4+	-
Kaptin	5"	3+	4+	5	4	2	3	6	4+	1

This model is armed with a snazzgun and stikkbombs.
One Flash Git in your kill team can be a Kaptin.

WARGEAR OPTIONS	• One Flash Git or Kaptin in your kill team may take a choppa. • Another Flash Git or Kaptin in your kill team may take a slugga. • One Flash Git or Kaptin in your kill team may take a gitfinda squig.
ABILITIES	**'Ere We Go:** Re-roll failed charge rolls for this model. **Gun-crazy Show-off:** After this model has shot in the Shooting phase, roll a D6. On a 6 the model can immediately shoot again, but can only target the nearest enemy model. **Gitfinda Squig:** Add 1 to hit rolls for shooting attacks made by a model with a gitfinda squig.
SPECIALISTS	**Leader** (Kaptin only), **Combat, Comms, Demolitions, Heavy, Veteran**
FACTION KEYWORD	Oʀᴋs
KEYWORDS	Fʀᴇᴇʙᴏᴏᴛᴇʀᴢ, Iɴꜰᴀɴᴛʀʏ, Fʟᴀsʜ Gɪᴛ

BOSS SNIKROT

NAME	M	WS	BS	S	T	W	A	Ld	Sv	Max
Boss Snikrot	6"	2+	5+	6	4	6	6	7	6+	1

This model is armed with Mork's Teeth and stikkbombs.
Only one of this model may be included on your command roster.

WEAPON	RANGE	TYPE	S	AP	D	ABILITIES
Mork's Teeth	Melee	Melee	User	-1	2	-

ABILITIES	**'Ere We Go:** Re-roll failed charge rolls for this model. **Terrifying Killer:** Subtract 1 from the Leadership characteristic of enemy models while they are within 3" of Boss Snikrot.
SPECIALISTS	Legendary Hunter (Level 3)
FACTION KEYWORD	ORKS
KEYWORDS	COMMANDER, INFANTRY, KOMMANDO, BOSS SNIKROT

RED SKULL KOMMANDOS

Orks Tactic
Boss Snikrot Aura Tactic

Use this Tactic at the start of the Fight phase if your kill team includes Boss Snikrot. That model gains the following aura ability until the end of the battle round:

As long as this model is not shaken, you can re-roll hit rolls of 1 for friendly **KOMMANDOS** within 6" of this model.

1 COMMAND POINT

ORKS	
MODEL	**POINTS PER MODEL**
Boss Snikrot (Level 3)	82
WARGEAR	**POINTS PER ITEM**
Mork's Teeth	0
Stikkbombs	0

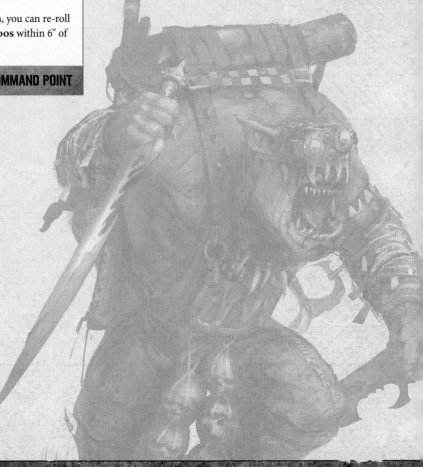

RANGED WEAPONS

WEAPON	RANGE	TYPE	S	AP	D	ABILITIES
Kustom shoota	18"	Assault 4	4	0	1	-
Snazzgun	24"	Heavy 3	6	-2	2	-

MELEE WEAPONS

WEAPON	RANGE	TYPE	S	AP	D	ABILITIES
Killsaw	Melee	Melee	x2	-4	2	When attacking with this weapon, you must subtract 1 from the hit roll. If a model is armed with two killsaws, add 1 to its Attacks characteristic.
Power stabba	Melee	Melee	User	-2	1	-

KILL TEAM

MODEL	POINTS PER MODEL (Does not include wargear)
Flash Git	23
- Kaptin	24
Meganob	37
- Boss Meganob	41
Nob	15
- Boss Nob	16
- Ammo Runt	3

RANGED WEAPONS

WEAPON	POINTS PER WEAPON
Kombi-weapon with rokkit launcha	3
Kombi-weapon with skorcha	7
Kustom shoota	0
Slugga	0
Snazzgun	0
Stikkbombs	0

MELEE WEAPONS

WEAPON	POINTS PER WEAPON
Big choppa	3
Choppa	1
Killsaw (single/pair)	5/7
Power klaw	5
Power stabba	1

OTHER WARGEAR

WEAPON	POINTS PER ITEM
Cybork body	5
Gitfinda squig	4

T'AU EMPIRE

Originating upon the Eastern Fringe of the galaxy, the T'au Empire is a young and dynamic xenos civilisation that is spreading across the stars at a rapacious pace. Prizing technology, innovation and unity, the T'au proselytise their doctrine of service to the Greater Good, enforcing their words with highly advanced weaponry.

The T'au Empire maintains a rigid caste system, with different facets of their civilisation taking responsibility for different areas of the empire's function. Warfare and expansion of colonial borders falls to the Fire caste. Trained in academies dotted across the inner sept worlds, these warriors are fully indoctrinated into the tenets of the Greater Good. They live to serve the T'au Empire, and turn all their discipline, determination and rigorous training to the furtherance of its goals. Amongst the Fire caste, the aspiration to rise through the ranks is a driving force, and the empire's elite kill teams are populated by driven heroes whose selfless devotion to their species makes them dangerous foes indeed.

One of the greatest advantages enjoyed by elite T'au operatives is their access to the full might of the empire's ever-advancing military technologies, from AI-controlled support drones and remote-strike missile systems, to multispectral targeting arrays and a bewildering range of ferociously powerful firearms. Yet the most deadly, iconic and prestigious item of equipment is the battlesuit.

Though the T'au Empire boasts many marks of these mechanised combat-suits, still the most enduringly popular is the XV8 Crisis Battlesuit. Standing over twice the height of a T'au Fire Warrior, these powered, articulated and fully enclosed suits of armour greatly enhance their operator's effectiveness in battle. They mount jet thrusters that allow the pilot to drop into battle from on high, and to traverse the combat engagement area in rocketing leaps. The suits' multiple hard points enable them to mount varying configurations of weaponry, as well as dedicated support systems that wreathe the suits in energy shields, guide their targeting, or allow them to control swarms of Drones while in combat. A small team of Crisis Battlesuits can swiftly and decisively annihilate far larger enemy forces through agility, firepower and durability, before pressing on to their next target.

Rarer and more experimental marks of battlesuit are sometimes issued to courageous T'au Commanders. This allows for final testing of the units in real combat scenarios, while also greatly enhancing these already skilled warriors' effectiveness. Some Commanders favour the XV85 Enforcer Battlesuit for its durability and ballistic punch. Able to mount a quartet of weapons or support systems, and tough enough to shrug off the majority of enemy attacks, the Enforcer allows a T'au Commander to dissect enemy kill teams with the precise application of overwhelming firepower.

Amongst the Fire caste there are those individuals whose skills and exploits are so exceptional that they have become figures of propaganda and warrior folklore both. Perhaps the most controversial of these figures is Commander Darkstrider. An officer amongst the Pathfinder cadres, this warrior's unconventional tactics and disregard for protocol have won him countless engagements but few friends amongst the Fire caste's upper echelons.

T'AU EMPIRE KILL TEAMS

If every model in your kill team has the T'AU EMPIRE Faction keyword, you can use T'au Empire Tactics.

MANTA STRIKE

T'au Empire Tactic

Use this Tactic at the end of the Movement phase. Choose up to three models that are any combination of BATTLESUITS that are not INFANTRY but can FLY, MV1 Gun Drones, MV4 Shield Drones or MV7 Marker Drones from your kill team that were set up in Reserve and set them up anywhere on the battlefield that is more than 5" away from any enemy models.

1 COMMAND POINT

STEALTHY HUNTERS

T'au Empire Tactic

Use this Tactic at the beginning of the first battle round. Choose up to three KROOT CARNIVORE models from your kill team that were set up in Reserve and set them up anywhere on the battlefield that is more than 9" away from any enemy deployment zone.

1 COMMAND POINT

NEUROWEB SYSTEM JAMMER

T'au Empire Tactic

Use this Tactic at the start of the Shooting phase. Pick an enemy model within 12" of a model from your kill team. Until the end of the phase, that model's controlling player must subtract 1 from hit rolls made for that model.

1 COMMAND POINT

STEALTH FIELDS

T'au Empire Tactic

Use this Tactic at the beginning of the first battle round. Choose up to three XV25 STEALTH BATTLESUIT models from your kill team that were set up in Reserve and set them up anywhere on the battlefield that is more than 9" away from any enemy deployment zone.

1 COMMAND POINT

FOCUSED FIRE

T'au Empire Tactic

Use this Tactic after a model from your kill team inflicts an unsaved wound on an enemy model in the Shooting phase. For the rest of the phase, you can add 1 to wound rolls for attacks made by other models from your kill team that target the same enemy model, so long the attacking model is within 2" of the model that inflicted the wound.

1 COMMAND POINT

SUPPORT TURRET REPLACEMENT

T'au Empire Tactic

Use this Tactic at the end of the Movement phase. Pick a friendly FIRE WARRIOR or FIRE WARRIOR BREACHER model whose DS8 Tactical Support Turret has been removed from the battlefield. You may immediately set up a new DS8 Tactical Support Turret within 2" of that model.

2 COMMAND POINTS

COMMANDER IN XV85 ENFORCER BATTLESUIT

NAME	M	WS	BS	S	T	W	A	Ld	Sv	Max
Commander in XV85 Enforcer Battlesuit	8"	3+	2+	5	5	6	4	9	3+	1

This model is armed with a burst cannon and missile pod.

WARGEAR OPTIONS	• This model may replace its burst cannon and missile pod with two items from the *Ranged Weapons* and/or *Support Systems* lists (pg 109). • This model may take two additional items from the *Ranged Weapons* and/or *Support Systems* lists (pg 109).
ABILITIES	**For the Greater Good:** When an enemy model declares a charge against a model from your kill team, models from your kill team with this ability within 6" of one of the charging model's targets may fire Overwatch as if they were also targeted. Once a model has done so, they cannot fire Overwatch or Retreat for the rest of the phase.
SPECIALISTS	**Fortitude**, **Leadership**, **Logistics**, **Shooting**, **Strategist**, **Strength**
FACTION KEYWORD	T'AU EMPIRE
KEYWORDS	BATTLESUIT, COMMANDER, XV85 ENFORCER, JET PACK, FLY

MASTER OF WAR

T'au Empire Tactic
Commander in XV85 Enforcer Battlesuit Aura Tactic

Use this Tactic at the start of the battle round if your kill team includes a Commander in XV85 Enforcer Battlesuit. Choose one of the following aura abilities. That model gains that ability until the end of the battle round:

Kauyon: As long as this model is not shaken, friendly models that begin the Movement phase within 3" of this model cannot move for any reason, but you can re-roll failed hit rolls for these models' attacks.

Mont'ka: As long as this model is not shaken, friendly models can shoot in the Shooting phase as if they had not moved in the preceding Movement phase whilst within 3" of this model, and you can add 1 to hit rolls for their shooting attacks that target enemy models that are not at long range.

You can only use this Tactic once per battle.

2 COMMAND POINTS

T'AU EMPIRE

MODEL	POINTS PER MODEL
Commander in XV85 Enforcer Battlesuit (Level 1)	62
Commander in XV85 Enforcer Battlesuit (Level 2)	82
Commander in XV85 Enforcer Battlesuit (Level 3)	102
Commander in XV85 Enforcer Battlesuit (Level 4)	127

WARGEAR	POINTS PER ITEM
Advanced targeting system	5
Airbursting fragmentation projector	6
Burst cannon	7
Counterfire defence system	5
Cyclic ion blaster	8
Drone controller	5
Early warning override	10
Flamer	4
Fusion blaster	20
Missile pod	17
Multi-tracker	5
Plasma rifle	7
Shield generator	20
Target lock	10
Velocity tracker	5

XV8 CRISIS BATTLESUIT

NAME	M	WS	BS	S	T	W	A	Ld	Sv	Max
XV8 Crisis Shas'ui	8"	5+	4+	5	5	3	2	7	3+	-
XV8 Crisis Shas'vre	8"	5+	4+	5	5	3	3	8	3+	1

This model is armed with a burst cannon.
One XV8 Crisis Battlesuit in your kill team can be an XV8 Crisis Shas'vre.

WARGEAR OPTIONS	• This model may replace its burst cannon with up to three items from the *Ranged Weapons* and/or *Support Systems* lists (pg 109). • Up to three **XV8 Crisis Battlesuit** models in your kill team may take an XV8-02 Crisis Iridium Battlesuit.
ABILITIES	**For the Greater Good:** When an enemy model declares a charge against a model from your kill team, models from your kill team with this ability within 6" of one of the charging model's targets may fire Overwatch as if they were also targeted. Once a model has done so, they cannot fire Overwatch or Retreat for the rest of the phase. **Bonding Knife Ritual:** You can subtract 1 from Nerve tests for XV8 Crisis Shas'uis or XV8 Crisis Shas'vres from your kill team within 3" of any other friendly models with this ability that are not shaken. **XV8-02 Crisis Iridium Battlesuit:** A model with an XV8-02 Crisis Iridium Battlesuit has a Save characteristic of 2+.
SPECIALISTS	**Leader** (XV8 Crisis Shas'vre only), **Comms**, **Demolitions**, **Heavy**, **Sniper**, **Veteran**
FACTION KEYWORD	**T'au Empire**
KEYWORDS	**Battlesuit, Jet Pack, Fly, XV8 Crisis Battlesuit**

KROOT CARNIVORE

NAME	M	WS	BS	S	T	W	A	Ld	Sv	Max
Kroot	7"	3+	4+	3	3	1	1	6	6+	-

This model is armed with a Kroot rifle.

SPECIALISTS	**Leader, Combat, Scout, Sniper, Veteran, Zealot**
FACTION KEYWORD	**T'au Empire**
KEYWORDS	**Kroot, Infantry, Kroot Carnivore**

DARKSTRIDER

NAME	M	WS	BS	S	T	W	A	Ld	Sv	Max
Darkstrider	7"	3+	2+	3	3	5	3	8	5+	1

This model is armed with a markerlight, pulse carbine and photon grenades.
Only one of this model may be included on your command roster.

ABILITIES	**For the Greater Good:** When an enemy model declares a charge against a model from your kill team, models from your kill team with this ability within 6" of one of the charging model's targets may fire Overwatch as if they were also targeted. Once a model has done so, they cannot fire Overwatch or Retreat for the rest of the phase.
SPECIALISTS	Legendary Hunter (Level 2)
FACTION KEYWORD	T'AU EMPIRE
KEYWORDS	COMMANDER, INFANTRY, DARKSTRIDER

FIGHTING RETREAT

T'au Empire Tactic
Darkstrider Aura Tactic

Use this Tactic at the start of the Shooting phase if your kill team includes Darkstrider. That model gains the following aura ability until the end of the battle round:

As long as this model is not shaken, friendly models within 3" of this model in the Shooting phase may attack with ranged weapons even if they Fell Back or Retreated this battle round.

2 COMMAND POINTS

T'AU EMPIRE	
MODEL	**POINTS PER MODEL**
Darkstrider (Level 2)	39
WARGEAR	**POINTS PER ITEM**
Markerlight	0
Photon grenades	0
Pulse carbine	0

STRUCTURAL ANALYSER

T'au Empire Tactic
Darkstrider Aura Tactic

Use this Tactic at the start of the Shooting phase if your kill team includes Darkstrider. That model gains the following aura ability until the end of the battle round:

Pick an enemy model visible to Darkstrider. As long as Darkstrider is not shaken, add 1 to wound rolls for shooting attacks made by friendly models within 6" of Darkstrider in the Shooting phase that target the enemy model you picked.

1 COMMAND POINT

RANGED WEAPONS

WEAPON	RANGE	TYPE	S	AP	D	ABILITIES
Airbursting fragmentation projector	18"	Assault D6	4	0	1	This weapon can target models that are not visible to the bearer. If the target is not visible to the bearer, a 6 is required for a successful hit roll, irrespective of the firing model's Ballistic Skill or any modifiers.
Cyclic ion blaster	When attacking with this weapon, choose one of the profiles below.					
- Standard	18"	Assault 3	7	-1	1	-
- Overcharge	18"	Assault 3	8	-1	D3	If you make one or more unmodified hit rolls of 1, the bearer suffers a mortal wound after all of this weapon's shots have been resolved.
Flamer	8"	Assault D6	4	0	1	This weapon automatically hits its target.
Kroot rifle	This weapon can be used as a ranged weapon and a melee weapon. When making shooting attacks or firing Overwatch with this weapon, use the ranged profile; when making close combat attacks, use the melee profile.					
- Ranged	24"	Rapid Fire 1	4	0	1	-
- Melee	Melee	Melee	+1	0	1	-
Plasma rifle	24"	Rapid Fire 1	6	-3	1	-

SUPPORT SYSTEMS (A model cannot have more than one of the same Support System.)

SUPPORT SYSTEM	ABILITIES
Advanced targeting system	Improve the AP characteristic of this model's ranged weapons by 1 (e.g. an AP of 0 becomes -1, an AP of -1 becomes -2).
Counterfire defence system	Re-roll failed hit rolls for this model's shooting attacks when it fires Overwatch.
Drone controller	Add 1 to the hit rolls of attacks made by **DRONE** models within 6" of any friendly models (other than shaken models) with a drone controller.
Early warning override	If any enemy models are set up within 12" of this model during a phase, and this model is not shaken, then at the end of the phase this model may immediately shoot at one of those models as if it were your Shooting phase, but you must subtract 1 from hit rolls when resolving these shots.
Multi-tracker	Re-roll hit rolls of 1 in the Shooting phase for this model if it targets more than one model when it uses a ranged weapon.
Shield generator	This model has a 4+ invulnerable save.
Target lock	This model does not suffer the penalty for moving and firing Heavy weapons, or for Advancing and firing Assault weapons. The model can also Advance and fire Rapid Fire weapons, but you must subtract 1 from its hit rolls when it does so.
Velocity tracker	Add 1 to hit rolls for this model's ranged attacks that target a model that can **FLY**.

KILL TEAM

MODEL	POINTS PER MODEL (Does not include wargear)
Kroot Carnivore	6
XV8 Crisis Battlesuit	-
- XV8 Crisis Shas'ui	32
- XV8 Crisis Shas'vre	33

OTHER WARGEAR

WARGEAR	POINTS PER ITEM
Advanced targeting system	5
Counterfire defence system	3
Drone controller	3
Early warning override	5
Multi-tracker	3
Shield generator	10
Target lock	5
Velocity tracker	3
XV8-02 Crisis Iridium Battlesuit	10

RANGED WEAPONS

WEAPON	POINTS PER WEAPON
Airbursting fragmentation projector	3
Burst cannon	4
Cyclic ion blaster	8
Flamer	4
Fusion blaster	8
Kroot rifle	0
Missile pod	10
Plasma rifle	3

TYRANIDS

The Tyranids swarm across the galaxy in vast hive fleets, driven by a terrifying gestalt intelligence known as the Hive Mind. Their only goal is to devour all biomass in their path and use it to fuel the spawning of fresh waves of horrific xenos war-beasts to unleash upon the next world they invade.

To battle the Tyranids is to endure the furious and relentless assault of a fractal super-predator, its fangs and talons the myriad organisms that it hurls, wave-on-wave, into the fight. The Tyranids have no conventional technology whatsoever. Instead, everything they put into the field – from their swarming foot soldiers to their looming siege-beasts and all of the weapons they wield – is biological in nature. The Tyranids see not enemy armies but herds of prey, and they scuttle, slither, lumber and fly into battle with absolutely no concept of fear, pain, fatigue, mercy or doubt. From the smallest biomass-devouring entity to the largest commanding node-beast, every Tyranid is wholly slaved to the will of the Hive Mind and attacks ferociously and without pause, even unto its own destruction.

One facet of the Tyranids' way of war is that, whenever a crucial strategic demand arises, the Hive Mind can simply fashion creatures ideally armed and adapted to fulfil it and then hurl them into battle. Whether it be assassinating key enemy commanders, breaking into lynchpin strongholds to bring down the prey's defences, or throwing up a shield of chitin and blades to protect its swarms' leader-beasts, the Hive Mind always has bio-warriors perfect for the task at hand.

When on the attack, Tyranid Raveners are particularly deadly. Able to tunnel through bedrock and ferrocrete foundations with terrifying speed, these blade-limbed horrors burst up from below to turn command bunkers into slaughterhouses and drag their prey's leaders screaming into the depths. Even more accomplished in assassination duties is the strain of Lictor known as the Deathleaper. Once this agile chameleonic killer has its prey's biospoor, it pursues them tirelessly and inescapably until, at last, it is able to crack open their cranium and devour their brain – and the knowledge contained therein.

When the prey fights back, the Hive Mind instead deploys its guard organisms to blunt the enemy's fury and destroy their attacking forces. Should the foe target the leader-beasts that act as nodes for the Hive Mind's will, they encounter living shield-walls of Tyrant Guard. These hulking monsters are covered with layer upon layer of chitinous armour that render them nigh-impervious to blade strikes and small arms fire, while their crushing claws and scything talons make short work of anyone foolish enough to come close.

Hive Guard, by comparison, are deployed primarily to defend the huge biomechanical digestion structures the Hive Mind raises during the latter stages of an invasion. Hive Guard are centauroid weapon-beasts whose impaler cannons can maintain a ferocious rate of fire, their vicious ammunition shards punching through armour, flesh and bone with ease, and even swerving in mid-air to hunt down those prey cowering in cover.

TYRANIDS KILL TEAMS

If every model in your kill team has the TYRANIDS Faction keyword, you can use Tyranids Tactics.

DEATH FROM BELOW

Tyranids Tactic

Use this Tactic at the end of the Movement phase. Choose up to three RAVENER models from your kill team that were set up in Reserve and set them up anywhere on the battlefield that is more than 5" away from any enemy models.

1 COMMAND POINT

PREDATORY LEAP

Tyranids Tactic

Use this Tactic before making a charge roll for a model from your kill team. Treat that model as if it could FLY when making its charge move.

1 COMMAND POINT

IMPLANT ATTACK

Tyranids Tactic

Use this Tactic before an Injury roll is made for an enemy model that was reduced to 0 wounds by a model from your kill team in the Fight phase. Apply a +2 modifier to the Injury roll.

2 COMMAND POINTS

LEGACY OF YMGARL

Tyranids Tactic

Use this Tactic when you choose a Genestealer in your kill team to fight in the Fight phase. Re-roll failed wound rolls for that model until the end of the phase.

1 COMMAND POINT

ADRENALINE SURGE

Tyranids Tactic

Use this Tactic at the end of the Fight phase. Pick a model from your kill team. That model can immediately fight an additional time.

2 COMMAND POINTS

RAPID REGENERATION

Tyranids Tactic

Use this Tactic when a model from your kill team is taken out of action. Roll a D6. On a 4+ that model is treated as if it had suffered a flesh wound instead.

2 COMMAND POINTS

SINGLE-MINDED ANNIHILATION

Tyranids Tactic

Use this Tactic after a model from your kill team shoots in the Shooting phase. You can immediately shoot an additional time with that model. This Tactic costs 1 Command Point to use, or 2 Command Points if used on a TYRANID WARRIOR or RAVENER, or 3 Command Points if used on a HIVE GUARD.

1-3 COMMAND POINTS

DEATHLEAPER

NAME	M	WS	BS	S	T	W	A	Ld	Sv	Max
Deathleaper	9"	2+	4+	6	4	6	4	10	5+	1

This model is armed with flesh hooks, grasping talons and rending claws.
Only one of this model may be included on your command roster.

ABILITIES	**It's After Me!:** You can re-roll hit and wound rolls in the Fight phase for any of Deathleaper's attacks that target enemy **COMMANDERS**. In addition, Deathleaper can make a charge attempt when it is set up from Reserve, though if it does so you may only roll a single D6 (rather than 2D6) for the charge roll.
SPECIALISTS	Legendary Hunter (Level 4)
FACTION KEYWORD	**TYRANIDS**
KEYWORDS	**COMMANDER, INFANTRY, LICTOR, DEATHLEAPER**

MELT INTO THE SHADOWS

Tyranids Tactic

Use this Tactic at the beginning of the battle round if Deathleaper is on the battlefield and not shaken. Until the end of the battle round, that model cannot make any charge attempts, but your opponent must subtract 1 from hit rolls for attacks that target that model.

1 COMMAND POINT

TYRANIDS	
MODEL	POINTS PER MODEL
Deathleaper (Level 4)	70
WARGEAR	POINTS PER ITEM
Flesh hooks	0
Grasping talons	0
Rending claws	0

TYRANT GUARD

NAME	M	WS	BS	S	T	W	A	Ld	Sv	Max
Tyrant Guard	7"	3+	4+	5	5	3	3	6	3+	-

This model is armed with rending claws and scything talons.

WARGEAR OPTIONS	• This model may replace its scything talons with crushing claws or a lash whip and bonesword. • This model may take toxin sacs and/or adrenal glands.

ABILITIES	**Instinctive Behaviour:** Unless this model is within 24" of a friendly **SYNAPSE** model, you must subtract 1 from any hit rolls made for it when shooting any target other than the nearest visible enemy model, and subtract 2 from charge rolls made for it if it declares a charge against any model other than the nearest enemy model. **Shieldwall:** Roll a dice each time a **COMMANDER** loses a wound whilst they are within 3" of any friendly models with this ability; on a 2+ choose one of these models to intercept that hit – the Commander does not lose a wound but the model you chose suffers a mortal wound.	**Blind Rampage:** From the end of a phase in which a friendly **COMMANDER** is taken out of action, until the end of the battle, this model's Weapon Skill characteristic becomes 4+ and its Attacks characteristic becomes 4. **Adrenal Glands:** If a model has adrenal glands, add 1" to the distance it can move when it Advances or charges. **Toxin Sacs:** Any wound rolls of 6+ in the Fight phase for a model with toxin sacs cause 1 additional damage.

SPECIALISTS	Combat, Veteran, Zealot
FACTION KEYWORD	**TYRANIDS**
KEYWORDS	**INFANTRY, TYRANT GUARD**

HIVE GUARD

NAME	M	WS	BS	S	T	W	A	Ld	Sv	Max
Hive Guard	5"	4+	3+	4	5	3	2	7	4+	-

This model is armed with an impaler cannon.

WARGEAR OPTIONS	• This model may replace its impaler cannon with a shockcannon. • This model may take toxin sacs and/or adrenal glands.

ABILITIES	**Instinctive Behaviour:** Unless this model is within 24" of a friendly **SYNAPSE** model, you must subtract 1 from any hit rolls made for it when shooting any target other than the nearest visible enemy model, and subtract 2 from charge rolls made for it if it declares a charge against any model other than the nearest enemy model.	**Adrenal Glands:** If a model has adrenal glands, add 1" to the distance it can move when it Advances or charges. **Toxin Sacs:** Any wound rolls of 6+ in the Fight phase for a model with toxin sacs cause 1 additional damage.

SPECIALISTS	Heavy, Sniper, Veteran
FACTION KEYWORD	**TYRANIDS**
KEYWORDS	**INFANTRY, HIVE GUARD**

RAVENER

NAME	M	WS	BS	S	T	W	A	Ld	Sv	Max
Ravener	12"	3+	4+	4	4	3	4	5	5+	-

This model is armed with two pairs of scything talons.

WARGEAR OPTIONS	• This model may replace one of its pairs of scything talons with rending claws. • This model may take a devourer, deathspitter or spinefists.
ABILITIES	**Instinctive Behaviour:** Unless this model is within 24" of a friendly **SYNAPSE** model, you must subtract 1 from any hit rolls made for it when shooting any target other than the nearest visible enemy model, and subtract 2 from charge rolls made for it if it declares a charge against any model other than the nearest enemy model.
SPECIALISTS	Combat, Scout, Veteran
FACTION KEYWORD	**TYRANIDS**
KEYWORDS	**INFANTRY, RAVENER**

RANGED WEAPONS

WEAPON	RANGE	TYPE	S	AP	D	ABILITIES
Impaler cannon	36"	Heavy 2	8	-2	D3	This weapon can be fired at models that are not visible to the bearer. If the target is not visible to the bearer, a 6 is required for a successful hit roll, irrespective of the firing model's Ballistic Skill or any modifiers.
Shockcannon	36"	Assault D3	7	-1	D3	-

MELEE WEAPONS

WEAPON	RANGE	TYPE	S	AP	D	ABILITIES
Crushing claws	Melee	Melee	x2	-3	D3	When attacking with this weapon, you must subtract 1 from the hit roll.

KILL TEAM

MODEL	POINTS PER MODEL (Does not include wargear)
Hive Guard	35
Ravener	15
Tyrant Guard	32

MELEE WEAPONS

WEAPON	POINTS PER WEAPON
Crushing claws	7
Lash whip and bonesword	1
Rending claws	1
Scything talons	0

RANGED WEAPONS

WEAPON	POINTS PER WEAPON
Deathspitter	5
Devourer (Ravener)	3
Impaler cannon	0
Shockcannon	0
Spinefists	2

OTHER WARGEAR

WARGEAR	POINTS PER ITEM
Adrenal glands	1
Toxin sacs	1

GENESTEALER CULTS

The Genestealer Cults are a canker growing within the heart of Imperial society. Upon countless worlds there exist cells of xenophile cultists, their biology tainted by Tyranid genetic materials, their lives utterly dedicated to throwing off their Imperial shackles in the name of their cult's monstrous Patriarch.

Amongst the ranks of the Genestealer Cults there are those individuals chosen for greater things. Though even the lowliest Neophyte still takes pride in their role, and strives willingly unto death if needs be to make their contribution to the cause, there can be no denying that not all the Patriarch's servants are created equal. To certain strains of fourth-generation hybrids fall tasks of such vital importance that they form kill teams in their own right, or else are assigned entire warbands of specialist operatives to ensure their safety while they complete their great works.

The Clamavus is an information manipulator and propaganda mouthpiece supreme. He is bonded directly to the gestalt mind of the cult through his connection to the Patriarch. This allows the Clamavus

to overload his enemies' minds with an unstoppable psionic bombardment, while simultaneously inspiring the faithful to deeds of great heroism and self-sacrifice. Coupled with his ability to steal audio transmissions from enemy comms channels and selectively feed them back through his own, this makes the Clamavus a deadly foe indeed.

The Locus is a bodyguard and arch-protector. This being maintains an unnatural level of stillness, escaping his enemies' notice through unassuming dress and passive demeanour. Yet should any threaten his charge, the Locus strikes their heads from their shoulders with his finely honed blades, or throws back his robes and reveals the monstrous array of limbs beneath before tearing his enemies apart.

Some of these cult champions fight their wars from well behind the lines. The Biophagus, for example, is a master of biotoxins and cruel experimentation. When not spreading the cult's taint through all available vectors, he perfects lethal poisons and potent xenosteroids that can be used to inflict hideous deaths upon the enemy, or enhance his comrades' combat capabilities. The Nexos, meanwhile, is an infocyte, voraciously assimilating floods of tactical data absorbed directly from the cult's faithful and constructing a grand strategic picture in his throbbing cerebrum. The process is painful and exhausting, but the Nexos does not shy from his duties, for his role is vital in the coordination of the cult's uprising.

Then there are those gun-toting warriors who fight for the cult by striking directly at the foe. The Sanctus is a loner and an assassin. He hunts down those the Patriarch wishes to see dead and slays them with his atrophic blade or a silenced needle-rifle capable of delivering lethal biotoxins to even the most well-defended target. Where the Sanctus fights from the shadows, the Kelermorph does battle wherever he can be seen clearest; every aspect of this three-armed gunslinger is cynically calculated to evoke the most positive reaction in the human psyche. He swiftly becomes a folk hero who epitomises the uprising of the oppressed against the oppressor, while simultaneously wreaking havoc amidst the Patriarch's foes.

GENESTEALER CULTS KILL TEAMS

If every model in your kill team has the GENESTEALER CULTS Faction keyword, you can use Genestealer Cults Tactics.

SEISMIC BLAST

Genestealer Cults Tactic

Use this Tactic when you choose a model in your kill team to shoot with the short-wave profile of a seismic cannon. If an attack for the weapon hits, roll a dice for each other model within 2" of the target model. On a 5+ that model is shaken.

2 COMMAND POINTS

MESMERISING GAZE

Genestealer Cults Tactic

Use this Tactic at the beginning of the Fight phase. Pick an enemy model within 1" of a model (other than a shaken model) from your kill team and roll a dice. On a 4+ subtract 1 from that model's Attacks characteristic (to a minimum of 1) until the end of the phase.

1 COMMAND POINT

ACIDIC SPIT

Genestealer Cults Tactic

Use this Tactic at the beginning of the Shooting phase. Pick an enemy model within 1" of a model (other than a shaken model) from your kill team and roll a dice. On a 5+ that enemy model suffers 1 mortal wound.

1 COMMAND POINT

RAISE THE ICON

Genestealer Cults Tactic

Use this Tactic at the start of the Fight phase. Pick a model from your kill team equipped with a cult icon. Increase the range of that model's Cult Icon ability to 12" until the end of the phase.

1 COMMAND POINT

I LIKE TO KEEP THIS HANDY...

Genestealer Cults Tactic

Use this Tactic at the start of the Shooting phase. Pick a model from your kill team armed with a shotgun. Change the shotgun's Type to Pistol 2 until the end of the phase.

1 COMMAND POINT

TOXIN GLAND

Genestealer Cults Tactic

Use this Tactic when you pick a HYBRID METAMORPH from your kill team to fight in the Fight phase. Add 1 to wound rolls for that model's rending claw or metamorph talon until the end of the phase.

1 COMMAND POINT

SANCTUS

NAME	M	WS	BS	S	T	W	A	Ld	Sv	Max
Sanctus	6"	2+	2+	3	3	4	4	8	5+	1

This model is armed with a silencer sniper rifle and accompanied by a Soulsight Familiar which attacks using its Familiar claws.

WEAPON	RANGE	TYPE	S	AP	D	ABILITIES
Silencer sniper rifle	36"	Heavy 1	4	-1	D3	A model firing this weapon does not suffer the penalty to hit rolls for the target being at long range. If you roll a wound roll of 6+ for this weapon, it inflicts a mortal wound in addition to its normal damage. If a PSYKER loses any wounds as a result of this weapon's attacks, after all of this weapon's attacks have been resolved that model suffers Perils of the Warp.
Familiar claws	Melee	Melee	4	0	1	When this model fights, you cannot choose to use this weapon. After this model fights, you can make 2 additional attacks, using this weapon.
Sanctus bio-dagger	Melee	Melee	1	-2	2	Each time the bearer fights, it can make 1 additional attack with this weapon. In addition, this weapon wounds on a 2+.

WARGEAR OPTIONS	• This model may replace its silencer sniper rifle with a Sanctus bio-dagger.
ABILITIES	**Cult Ambush:** After deployment but before the first battle round, roll a D6 for this model. On a 5+ this model can immediately move up to 6".
	Camo Cloak: When an opponent makes a hit roll for a shooting attack that targets a model equipped with a camo cloak, and that model is obscured, that hit roll suffers an additional -1 modifier.
	Soulsight Familiar: Hit rolls for this model's ranged attacks do not suffer any penalty for the target being obscured.
SPECIALISTS	**Melee, Shooting, Stealth**
FACTION KEYWORD	**GENESTEALER CULTS**
KEYWORDS	**COMMANDER, INFANTRY, SANCTUS**

CULT ASSASSIN

Genestealer Cults Tactic

Use this Tactic at the beginning of the first battle round if a SANCTUS from your kill team is on the battlefield and not shaken. That model can immediately make a ranged attack as if it were the Shooting phase.

2 COMMAND POINTS

GENESTEALER CULTS	
MODEL	**POINTS PER MODEL**
Sanctus (Level 1)	33
Sanctus (Level 2)	38
Sanctus (Level 3)	53
Sanctus (Level 4)	73
WARGEAR	**POINTS PER ITEM**
Familiar claws	0
Sanctus bio-dagger	20
Silencer sniper rifle	0

KELERMORPH

NAME	M	WS	BS	S	T	W	A	Ld	Sv	Max
Kelermorph	6"	3+	2+	3	3	4	3	8	5+	1

This model is armed with three liberator autostubs and a cultist knife.

WEAPON	RANGE	TYPE	S	AP	D	ABILITIES
Liberator autostub	12"	Pistol 1	4	-1	2	-
Cultist knife	Melee	Melee	User	0	1	Each time the bearer fights, it can make 1 additional attack with this weapon.

ABILITIES	
	Cult Ambush: After deployment but before the first battle round, roll a D6 for this model. On a 5+ this model can immediately move up to 6".
	Inspirational Deeds: If an enemy model is taken out of action by an attack made with this model's liberator autostubs, then until the end of the phase, re-roll hit rolls of 1 for models from your kill team whilst they are within 6" of this model.
	Lightning Reflexes: This model has a 5+ invulnerable save.
SPECIALISTS	Fortitude, Leadership, Stealth, Shooting
FACTION KEYWORD	GENESTEALER CULTS
KEYWORDS	TYRANIDS, INFANTRY, COMMANDER, KELERMORPH

BLAZE OF GLORY

Genestealer Cults Tactic
Kelermorph Tactic

Use this Tactic when you pick a **KELERMORPH** from your kill team to shoot in the Shooting phase. Instead of shooting normally, you can make a single attack with one of this model's ranged weapons against each enemy model within 8" that is an eligible target.

1 COMMAND POINT

GENESTEALER CULTS

MODEL	POINTS PER MODEL
Kelermorph (Level 1)	25
Kelermorph (Level 2)	30
Kelermorph (Level 3)	45
Kelermorph (Level 4)	65
WARGEAR	**POINTS PER ITEM**
Liberator autostub	0
Cultist knife	0

NEXOS

NAME	M	WS	BS	S	T	W	A	Ld	Sv	Max
Nexos	6"	3+	3+	3	3	4	3	8	5+	1

This model is armed with an autopistol.

| ABILITIES | **Cult Ambush:** After deployment but before the first battle round, roll a D6 for this model. On a 5+ this model can immediately move up to 6".

Strategic Coordinator: Whilst this model is on the battlefield and not shaken, you can re-roll any rolls of 1 when rolling for a model's Cult Ambush ability. In addition, if your kill team is Battle-forged, then as long as this model is on the battlefield and not shaken, roll a dice each time a player spends one or more Command Points. On a roll of 6, you gain 1 Command Point.

Unquestioning Loyalty: Roll a D6 each time you use the Look Out, Sir! Commander Tactic on this model. On a 2+, you gain a Command Point. |
|-----------|---|
| SPECIALISTS | Logistics, Strategist |
| FACTION KEYWORD | GENESTEALER CULTS |
| KEYWORDS | COMMANDER, INFANTRY, NEXOS |

CULT NEXOS

Genestealer Cults Tactic

Use this Tactic at the end of the Movement phase if a **NEXOS** from your kill team is on the battlefield and not shaken and you have any models in Reserve. Choose up to three models from your kill team that were set up in Reserve and set them up within 1" of the edge of the battlefield and more than 5" away from any enemy models.

1 COMMAND POINT

GENESTEALER CULTS

MODEL	POINTS PER MODEL
Nexos (Level 1)	32
Nexos (Level 2)	37
Nexos (Level 3)	52
Nexos (Level 4)	72
WARGEAR	**POINTS PER ITEM**
Autopistol	0

BIOPHAGUS

NAME	M	WS	BS	S	T	W	A	Ld	Sv	Max
Biophagus	6"	3+	3+	3	3	4	3	8	5+	1
Alchemicus Familiar	6"	3+	6+	4	3	1	2	8	6+	1

A Biophagus is armed with an autopistol and injector goad.
If your kill team includes a Biophagus, it may also include an Alchemicus Familiar.

WEAPON	RANGE	TYPE	S	AP	D	ABILITIES
Injector goad	Melee	Melee	+1	0	D3	This weapon always wounds on a 2+. If a **COMMANDER** loses any wounds from this weapon, roll a D6 for it after all of this model's attacks have been resolved. If the result is higher than the Wounds characteristic of the **COMMANDER**, it suffers D3 mortal wounds.

ABILITIES	
	Cult Ambush: After deployment but before the first battle round, roll a D6 for this model. On a 5+ this model can immediately move up to 6".
	Familiar: Models do not suffer any penalty to their Nerve tests for a friendly **FAMILIAR** being out of action.
	Unquestioning Loyalty: Roll a D6 each time you use the Look Out, Sir! Commander Tactic on this model. On a 2+, you gain a Command Point.
SPECIALISTS	Logistics, Strategist
FACTION KEYWORD	**GENESTEALER CULTS**
KEYWORDS	**COMMANDER, INFANTRY, BIOPHAGUS** (Alchemicus Familiar is **INFANTRY, FAMILIAR**)

GENOMIC ENHANCEMENT

Genestealer Cults Tactic

Use this Tactic at the end of the Movement phase if a **BIOPHAGUS** from your kill team is on the battlefield and not shaken. Choose a friendly **ABERRANT** model within 2" of the **BIOPHAGUS**, and increase its Strength, Toughness or Attacks characteristic by 1 until the end of the mission. You cannot choose the same **ABERRANT** twice with this Tactic.

1 COMMAND POINT

GENESTEALER CULTS	
MODEL	POINTS PER MODEL
Biophagus (Level 1)	29
Biophagus (Level 2)	34
Biophagus (Level 3)	49
Biophagus (Level 4)	69
Alchemicus Familiar	4
WARGEAR	POINTS PER ITEM
Autopistol	0
Injector goad	0

LOCUS

NAME	M	WS	BS	S	T	W	A	Ld	Sv	Max
Locus	6"	2+	3+	4	3	4	4	8	5+	1

This model is armed with Locus blades and a hypermorph tail.

WEAPON	RANGE	TYPE	S	AP	D	ABILITIES
Locus blades	Melee	Melee	User	-3	1	This weapon's Damage characteristic is 2 in a battle round in which this model charged, was charged or performed a Sudden Strike (see below).
Hypermorph tail	Melee	Melee	User	-1	1	Each time the bearer fights, it can make 1 additional attack with this weapon.

ABILITIES	
	Cult Ambush: After deployment but before the first battle round, roll a D6 for this model. On a 5+ this model can immediately move up to 6".
	Neurotraumal Rod: Your opponent must add 1 to Nerve tests taken for enemy models that are within 3" of any models with this ability.
	Quicksilver Dodge: This model has a 5+ invulnerable save.
	Quicksilver Strike: If this fighter is within 1" of an enemy model at the beginning of the Fight phase, it is considered to have charged.
	Unquestioning Bodyguard: Roll a dice each time a Leader from your kill team loses a wound whilst they are within 3" of any friendly models with this ability; on a 2+ choose one of these models to intercept that hit – the Leader does not lose a wound but the model you chose suffers a mortal wound.
SPECIALISTS	Ferocity, Melee, Stealth
FACTION KEYWORD	GENESTEALER CULTS
KEYWORDS	COMMANDER, INFANTRY, LOCUS

SUDDEN STRIKE

Genestealer Cults Tactic

Use this Tactic at the end of the Movement phase if a **Locus** from your kill team is on the battlefield, is within 6" of an enemy model, did not Advance, Fall Back, Retreat, make a charge attempt or arrive from Reserve in this turn, and is not shaken or within 1" of an enemy model. The **Locus** can immediately make a pile-in move as described in the Fight phase, except that it can move up to 6" (rather than 3").

1 COMMAND POINT

GENESTEALER CULTS

MODEL	POINTS PER MODEL
Locus (Level 1)	66
Locus (Level 2)	81
Locus (Level 3)	96
Locus (Level 4)	121

WARGEAR	POINTS PER ITEM
Hypermorph tail	0
Locus blades	0

CLAMAVUS

NAME	M	WS	BS	S	T	W	A	Ld	Sv	Max
Clamavus	6"	3+	3+	3	3	4	3	8	5+	1

This model is armed with an autopistol.

ABILITIES	**Cult Ambush:** After deployment but before the first battle round, roll a D6 for this model. On a 5+ this model can immediately move up to 6".
	Scrambler Array: Enemy models that are set up on the battlefield from Reserve cannot be set up within 7" of this model.
	Unquestioning Loyalty: Roll a D6 each time you use the Look Out, Sir! Commander Tactic on this model. On a 2+, you gain a Command Point.
SPECIALISTS	Leadership, Strategist
FACTION KEYWORD	GENESTEALER CULTS
KEYWORDS	COMMANDER, INFANTRY, CLAMAVUS

PROCLAMATOR HAILER

Genestealer Cults Tactic
Clamavus Aura Tactic

Use this Tactic at the start of the battle round if your kill team includes a Clamavus. That model gains the following aura ability until the end of the phase:

As long as this model is not shaken, add 1 to all run and charge rolls made for models from your kill team that are within 6" of any friendly models with this ability, and subtract 1 from all Nerve tests made for models from your kill team that are within 6" of any friendly models with this ability.

1 COMMAND POINT

GENESTEALER CULTS

MODEL	POINTS PER MODEL
Clamavus (Level 1)	26
Clamavus (Level 2)	31
Clamavus (Level 3)	46
Clamavus (Level 4)	66
WARGEAR	POINTS PER ITEM
Autopistol	0

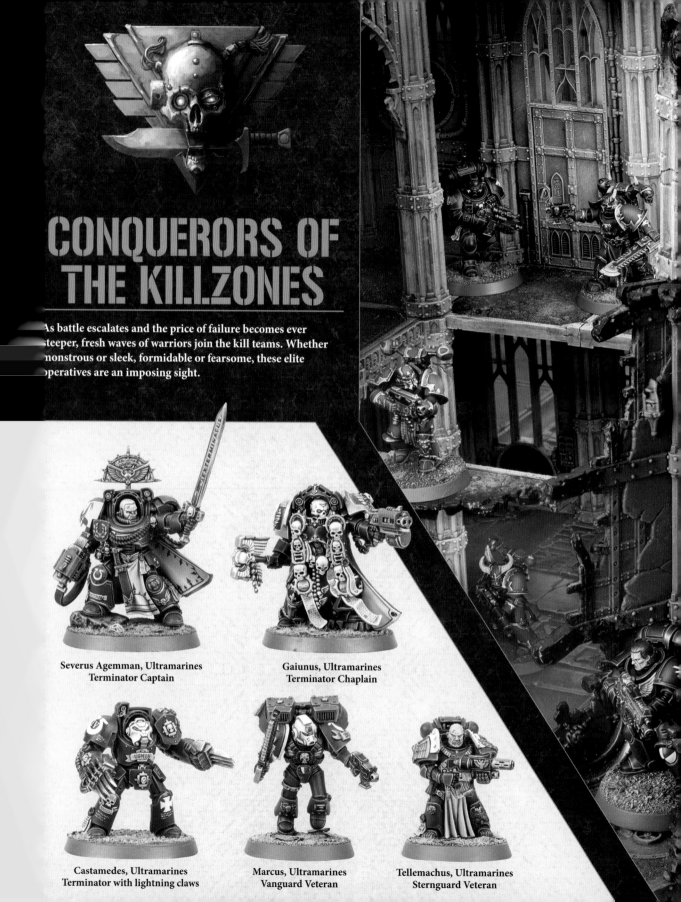

CONQUERORS OF THE KILLZONES

As battle escalates and the price of failure becomes ever steeper, fresh waves of warriors join the kill teams. Whether monstrous or sleek, formidable or fearsome, these elite operatives are an imposing sight.

Severus Agemman, Ultramarines Terminator Captain

Gaiunus, Ultramarines Terminator Chaplain

Castamedes, Ultramarines Terminator with lightning claws

Marcus, Ultramarines Vanguard Veteran

Tellemachus, Ultramarines Sternguard Veteran

Watched over by a graven image of Saint Sevastian the Grim, the elite operatives of the Dark Angels clash in battle with the twisted traitors of the Word Bearers Chaos Space Marine Legion.

Eldritch energies crackle through the air as the worshippers of the Machine God do battle with a band of Necron Lychguard beneath the shadow of a vast refinery complex.

Iodus, Ultramarines Suppressor Sergeant

Asclepius, Ultramarines Eliminator Sergeant

Sevastus Acheran, Ultramarines Captain in Phobos Armour

Tyrossus, Custodian Guard with sentinel blade

Prestylator Vence, Allarus Custodian with castellan axe

Krashlenkyn, Shield-Captain with sentinel blade

Ludoro, Brother-Captain with Nemesis force halberd

Asorphael, Paragon with Nemesis force sword

Rephas, Paladin with two Nemesis falchions

Nunk, Bullgryn with slabshield and grenadier gauntlet

Thrugg, Bone 'ead with ripper gun

Dronk, Ogryn with ripper gun

**Choragious, Black Legion
Dark Apostle**

**Vorash, Black Legion
Master of Possession**

**Hastus Asmodax, Black Legion
Master of Executions**

**Vraxos, Black Legion Terminator
with reaper autocannon**

**Kharagun, Black Legion Terminator
with chainaxe and combi-bolter**

**Rhaegus Bittersoul, Black Legion
Terminator Champion**

**Shurgholgh, Blightlord Terminator
with reaper autocannon**

**Spurrghul, Deathshroud Terminator
with manreaper**

**Gulgoth the Afflictor,
Lord of Contagion**

The highly trained soldiers of the Militarum Tempestus hold a trench-line against the terrifying onslaught of a kill team of Iron Warriors Heretic Astartes.

**Ishmalael the Sundered,
Black Legion Greater Possessed**

**Molthorox, the Spawn of Lies,
Black Legion Greater Possessed**

**Hasmadrax the Thrice-pledged,
Black Legion Possessed**

Nameless Prophets of Flesh Grotesque with flesh gauntlet

Gibberslit, Prophets of Flesh Wrack

Flayerling Threshh, Prophets of Flesh Acothyst

Stitchsinew, Prophets of Flesh Wrack

Amidst the swirling mists and toxic vapours of a predatory jungle, the ghost warriors of Craftworld Saim-Hann stride into battle against a suite

**Yillith,
Howling Banshee**

**Creighth,
Striking Scorpion Exarch**

**Illic Nightspear, the Walker
of the Hidden Path**

**Qelanaris,
Saim-Hann Spiritseer**

**Amnahep the Indomitable,
Lychguard**

**Telnohoc the Conqueror,
Lychguard**

**Ohmtec the Eliminator,
Triarch Praetorian**

**Senmonak the Ender,
Triarch Praetorian**

**Shas'vre Vior'la Kal'so, Crisis Battlesuit
with burst cannon**

**Darkstrider, the
Shadow That Strikes**

**Shas'o Vior'la Shen'shal, Commander in XV85
Enforcer Battlesuit**

Locus, Cult of the Four-armed Emperor

Clamavus, Cult of the Four-armed Emperor

Sanctus, Cult of the Four-armed Emperor

Nexos, Cult of the Four-armed Emperor

Led by the legendary Lictor designated as Deathleaper, a Tyranid kill team of Hive Fleet Leviathan closes in from all sides to tear apart a determined band of Ultramarines Vanguard Space Marines.

Kelermorph, Cult of the Four-armed Emperor

Biophagus, Cult of the Four-armed Emperor

Alchemicus Familiar

A cunning raid led by Boss Snikrot against an Imperial Munitorum cargo-dock is thrown into mayhem as the Wolf Guard Terminators of Winterfang's Rimeguard launch a sudden and bloody ambush.

**Uzwotz,
Evil Sunz Meganob**

**Boss Snikrot,
da Green Ghost**

**Grobber Drog,
Flash Git with snazzgun**

**Muzrok da Skull Smasha,
Goff Nob with choppa and slugga**

**Borzag Badfang, Goff Nob with
power klaw and slugga**

**Grubratz, Goff Nob with kombi-
weapon with skorcha**

**Zarbog da Basha, Goff Nob with
power klaw and slugga**

MISSIONS

Below you will find three examples of open play missions for games of Kill Team that include elite warriors, along with ideas to spark your imagination for other open play games. On pages 136-139 you will find four narrative play missions, and on pages 140-143 you will find four matched play missions.

- A group of diehards is sent deep behind enemy lines to intercept and eliminate an enemy commander.

- A kill team has failed to report in. The army's elite are sent to ascertain their fate.

- High command wants to put some newly requisitioned assets through their paces, and sends them on a dangerous mission.

- Seeking revenge for a teammate, an elite team defy orders and set out to hunt down an assassin.

- A lone operative is trapped behind enemy lines, which is unfortunate for the enemy – this terrifying warrior is more than a match for whole platoons.

- The army's most potent warriors are teleported into the heart of the enemy's command.

- A commander and their accompanying bodyguard are the only survivors of an ambush, and must fight through hostile territory to rejoin their army.

- A small band of warriors has been tasked with the defence of vital assets, but they are isolated and vastly outnumbered by the approaching enemy.

- A handful of elite killers has been wreaking havoc far from the front. A team of hunters is assembled to track them down and bring an end to their rampage.

- A chance meeting in no man's land between two scouts quickly escalates as all of the assets available on both sides are funnelled into the conflict.

- A macabre contest between elite forces leads to a mismatched team venturing into enemy territory, with each warrior determined to claim the most kills.

OPEN PLAY MISSION
DEEP STRIKE

A key defensive emplacement must be taken before the army can advance. High command authorises a dangerous strike directly onto the target, the better to overwhelm the defenders.

THE KILL TEAMS

This is a mission for two players. Choose which player will be the attacker and which will be the defender (roll off if you can't agree – the winner decides). Each player chooses a kill team.

THE BATTLEFIELD

Create the battlefield and set up terrain.

SCOUTING PHASE

Do not use the rules for the Scouting phase in this mission.

DEPLOYMENT

The defender sets up their kill team anywhere wholly within 6" of the centre of the battlefield. The attacker must set up all of their models in Reserve.

PRIORITY TARGET

When an attacker's model is set up from Reserve, it can be set up within 1" of the edge of the battlefield and more than 5" away from any enemy models. In addition, if the attacker's kill team is Battle-forged they gain an additional 1CP at the start of each battle round.

BATTLE LENGTH

The battle ends at the end of battle round 5.

VICTORY CONDITIONS

If, at the end of the battle, the defender's models are all shaken or out of action, the attacker wins. Otherwise, the defender wins.

OPEN PLAY MISSION
AGAINST THE ODDS

Cornered and vastly outnumbered, a small team of diehards prepares to overcome insurmountable odds or perish in the attempt.

THE KILL TEAMS

This is a mission for two players. Choose which player will be the attacker and which will be the defender (roll off if you can't agree – the winner decides). Each player chooses a kill team. The defender's kill team cannot include more than 5 models, and the attacker's kill team cannot include fewer than 10 models.

THE BATTLEFIELD

Create the battlefield and set up terrain.

SCOUTING PHASE

Resolve the Scouting phase as described in the *Kill Team Core Manual*.

DEPLOYMENT

The defender first sets up their entire kill team anywhere wholly within 5" of one of the short edges of the battlefield. The attacker then sets up their entire kill team anywhere wholly within 5" of the opposite edge of the battlefield.

BATTLE LENGTH

The battle ends at the end of battle round 5.

LAST STAND

Subtract 2 (rather than 1) from Nerve tests taken for the defender's models for each other model (do not count shaken models) from their kill team that is within 2".

VICTORY CONDITIONS

If, at the end of the battle, the defender's models are all shaken or out of action, the attacker wins. Otherwise, the defender wins.

OPEN PLAY MISSION
ALL OR NOTHING

As their fortunes in the ongoing war begin to wane, one side decides on an all-or-nothing gambit – a strike by their mightiest warriors to eliminate a key enemy strategist, in an attempt to change destiny.

THE KILL TEAMS

This is a mission for two players. Choose which player will be the attacker and which will be the defender (roll off if you can't agree – the winner decides). Each player chooses a kill team that may include one Commander.

THE BATTLEFIELD

Create the battlefield and set up terrain. The defender picks one half of the battlefield to be their deployment zone. The other half of the battlefield is the attacker's deployment zone.

SCOUTING PHASE

Do not use the rules for the Scouting phase in this mission.

DEPLOYMENT

The players alternate setting up models, starting with the defender. If a player runs out of models to set up, skip them. Continue setting up models until both players have set up their kill team. A player's models must be set up wholly within their deployment zone.

BATTLE LENGTH

The battle ends at the end of battle round 5.

VICTORY CONDITIONS

At the end of the battle, each player scores 3 victory points if the enemy Leader is out of action, 5 victory points if an enemy Commander is out of action, and

1 victory point for each other enemy model that is out of action. The player with the most victory points is the winner. If there is a tie, the defender wins if their Leader and/or Commander is still on the battlefield, otherwise the attacker wins.

NARRATIVE PLAY MISSION
VITAL SABOTAGE

There are some targets that are so vital to one side of a war that their opponents are willing to pay any price to see them destroyed. In one such case, a crack team is sent with orders to sabotage the target, and if necessary to die trying.

If you are playing a campaign, you can choose to play this mission instead of the Assassinate mission.

THE KILL TEAMS

This is a mission for two players. Choose which player will be the attacker and which will be the defender (roll off if you can't agree – the winner decides). Each player chooses a Faction keyword, and the players reveal their choices at the same time. Then each player chooses a Battle-forged kill team (see the *Kill Team Core Manual*) that only includes models with the Faction keyword they chose. Each kill team can cost up to 125 points.

THE BATTLEFIELD

Create the battlefield and set up terrain. An example of how you might do this is shown below. The defender places three objective markers in their deployment zone, and secretly numbers them 1, 2 and 3 (they should note this down, or if you are using Kill Team tokens, simply place the objective markers with the numbered side down). Each objective marker must be at least 6" from other objective markers and the edge of the battlefield.

SCOUTING PHASE

Resolve the Scouting phase as described in the *Kill Team Core Manual*.

DEPLOYMENT

The players alternate setting up models, starting with the defender. If a player runs out of models to set up, skip them. Continue setting up models until both players have set up their kill team. A player's models must be set up wholly within their deployment zone. Once the players have set up all of their models, deployment ends and the first battle round begins.

BATTLE LENGTH

Use the Variable Battle Length rules (pg 14) – the attacker rolls. In addition, if the target is sabotaged (see below), the battle ends.

SABOTAGE

If the attacker controls an objective marker at the end of a battle round, the defender must reveal its number. If it is numbered 1 or 2, remove it from the battlefield. If it is numbered 3, it is the target, and the attacker may attempt to sabotage it: to do so, they roll a D6 for each model (other than shaken models) from their kill team that is within 2" of that objective marker. On any roll of 6+, the target is sabotaged.

VICTORY CONDITIONS

If, at the end of the battle, the target has been sabotaged, the attacker wins. Otherwise, the defender wins.

RESOURCES

In a campaign game, if the attacker wins the mission, the defender loses 1 Intelligence and 1 Morale. If the defender wins the mission, the attacker loses 1 Morale.

ONLY THE MISSION MATTERS

Attacker Tactic

Use this Tactic at the end of the battle round, before making any dice rolls as described in Sabotage. Add 1 to the result of each dice you roll. You can only use this Tactic once per battle round.

2 COMMAND POINTS

DESPERATE DEFENDER

Defender Tactic

Use this Tactic at the end of the battle round, before determining which player controls which objectives. Choose a model from your kill team (other than a shaken model). That model is considered to be 2 models until the end of the battle round.

1 COMMAND POINT

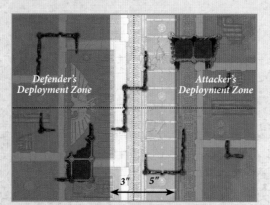

Defender's Deployment Zone   *Attacker's Deployment Zone*

3"   5"

NARRATIVE PLAY MISSION
SURROUNDED

Even the most experienced warriors can find themselves outmanoeuvred and surrounded. When this happens, there's little they can do other than hope that they are able to hold out until reinforcements arrive.

If you are playing a campaign, you can choose to play this mission instead of the Ambush mission.

THE KILL TEAMS

This is a mission for two players. Choose which player will be the attacker and which will be the defender (roll off if you can't agree – the winner decides). Each player chooses a Faction keyword, and the players reveal their choices at the same time. Then each player chooses a Battle-forged kill team (see the *Kill Team Core Manual*) that only includes models with the Faction keyword they chose. Each kill team can cost up to 125 points. The defender then splits their kill team into two parts, with at least one model in each part.

THE BATTLEFIELD

Create the battlefield and set up terrain. An example of how you might do this is shown below.

SCOUTING PHASE

Do not use the rules for the Scouting phase in this mission.

DEPLOYMENT

The defender sets up all of the models in one part of their kill team wholly within their deployment zone (they cannot set up any of these models in Reserve). Their remaining models are set up in Reserve. Then the attacker sets up one of their models wholly within one of their deployment zones, then another model wholly within their other deployment zone, and continues to alternate like this until all of their models have been set up. Once the players have set up all of their models, deployment ends and the first battle round begins.

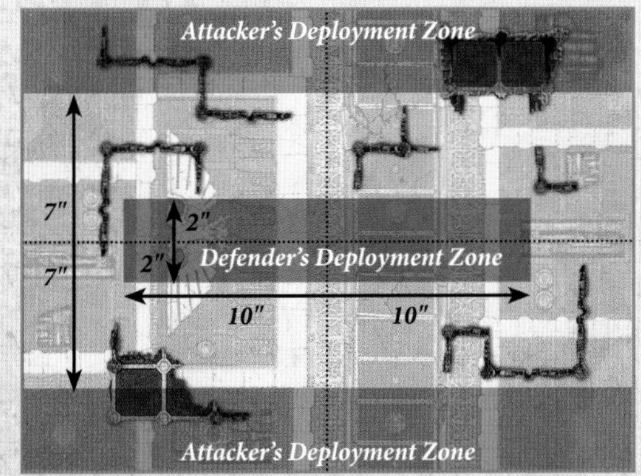

BATTLE LENGTH

Use the Variable Battle Length rules (pg 14) – the attacker rolls.

VICTORY CONDITIONS

If, at the end of the battle, all of the defender's models are out of action, shaken or in Reserve, the attacker wins. Otherwise, the defender wins.

AWAITING REINFORCEMENTS

The defender's models cannot be set up from Reserve in the first battle round. When a defender's model is set up from Reserve, it can be set up within 1" of the edge of the battlefield and more than 5" away from any enemy models.

RESOURCES

In a campaign game, if the attacker wins the mission, the defender loses 1 Morale and 1 Territory. If the defender wins the mission, the attacker loses 1 Materiel.

FINISH THEM

Attacker Tactic

Use this Tactic at the beginning of the Fight phase, if your Leader is on the battlefield and not shaken. Until the end of the phase, add 1 to wound rolls for attacks made by models from your kill team whilst they are within 3" of your Leader.

1 COMMAND POINT

VENGEFUL REINFORCEMENTS

Defender Tactic

Use this Tactic at the end of the Movement phase. You can choose any number of models from your kill team that were set up from Reserve in this battle round. Each of those models can make a charge attempt, but when they do so you only roll a D6 (rather than 2D6) for their charge roll.

1 COMMAND POINT

Attacker's Deployment Zone

7"

7"

2"

2"

Defender's Deployment Zone

10"

10"

Attacker's Deployment Zone

NARRATIVE PLAY MISSION
RAMPAGE

A group of dyed-in-the-wool killers have broken through enemy lines, and are now set to wreak havoc through the unsuspecting reserves. They must make their attack count – if they rampage for too long, they are sure to be cut off and eliminated.

If you are playing a campaign, you can choose to play this mission instead of the Ambush mission.

THE KILL TEAMS

This is a mission for two players. Choose which player will be the attacker and which will be the defender (roll off if you can't agree – the winner decides). Each player chooses a Faction keyword, and the players reveal their choices at the same time. Then each player chooses a Battle-forged kill team (see the *Kill Team Core Manual*) that only includes models with the Faction keyword they chose. Each kill team can cost up to 125 points. The attacker may include a Commander in their kill team, and the defender may not include a Commander in their kill team.

THE BATTLEFIELD

Create the battlefield and set up terrain. An example of how you might do this is shown below.

SCOUTING PHASE

Resolve the Scouting phase as described in the *Kill Team Core Manual*.

DEPLOYMENT

The players alternate setting up models, starting with the defender. The defender cannot set up any models in Reserve. If a player runs out of models to set up, skip them. Continue setting up models until both players have set up their kill team. A player's models must be set up wholly within their deployment zone. Once the players have set up all of their models, deployment ends and the first battle round begins.

BATTLE LENGTH

Use the Variable Battle Length rules (pg 14) – the attacker rolls. In addition, if at the end of a battle round all of the defender's models are shaken or out of action, or the attacker's Rampage count is 10 or more (see below), the battle ends.

RAMPAGE COUNT

Keep track of the attacker's rampage as described here:

EVENT	RAMPAGE COUNT
Defender's model is taken out of action	+X where X is that model's Wounds characteristic
End of a phase in which one or more of your models inflicted one or more mortal wounds	+1
Attacker makes an Injury roll for a defender's model with 3 or more dice	+1
End of the battle round (after checking if Rampage count is 10+)	-1
At the end of the battle round, any of the attacker's models are in their deployment zone	-1

VICTORY CONDITIONS

If the battle ends because all of the defender's models are shaken or out of action, or because the attacker's Rampage count is 10 or more, the attacker wins. Otherwise, the attacker scores a number of victory points equal to their Rampage count. The defender scores 2 victory points for each attacker's model that is out of action. The player with the most victory points is the winner. If there is a tie, the defender wins.

RESOURCES

In a campaign game, if the attacker wins the mission, the defender loses 1 Materiel and 1 Morale. If the defender wins the mission, the attacker loses 1 Morale.

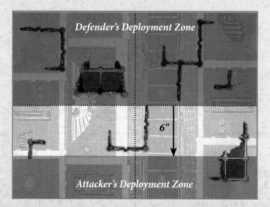

Defender's Deployment Zone

6"

Attacker's Deployment Zone

GORY SPECTACLE

Attacker Tactic

Use this Tactic when a defender's model is taken out of action. Add 1 to the Rampage count. You can only use this Tactic once per battle round.

1 COMMAND POINT

ESCAPE THE FACILITY

To their great shame, some elite warriors were captured. However, through ingenuity, opportunism or simple brute force, they have escaped, and must now fight their way out of the facility and its surroundings to freedom.

If you are playing a campaign, you can choose to play this mission instead of the Feint mission.

THE KILL TEAMS

This is a mission for two players. Choose which player will be the attacker and which will be the defender (roll off if you can't agree – the winner decides). Each player chooses a Faction keyword, and the players reveal their choices at the same time. Then each player chooses a Battle-forged kill team (see the *Kill Team Core Manual*) that only includes models with the Faction keyword they chose. Each kill team can cost up to 200 points. Each player may include a Commander in their kill team.

THE BATTLEFIELD

Create the battlefield and set up terrain. An example of how you might do this is shown below.

SCOUTING PHASE

Do not use the rules for the Scouting phase in this mission.

DEPLOYMENT

The attacker sets up all of their models wholly within their deployment zone (they cannot set up any models in Reserve). Then the defender sets up their models anywhere on the battlefield that is more than 8" from any of the attacker's models. Each of the defender's models must also be more than 4" from any of the defender's other models. Once the players have set up all of their models, deployment ends and the first battle round begins.

SENTRIES

In the first battle round, the defender's models on the battlefield cannot move (for any reason) or React. In addition, if at the beginning of the defender's turn in the Movement phase there are no attacker's models within 9" of a defender's model on the battlefield, that model cannot move (for any reason) or make any shooting attacks in that battle round. Commanders are not affected by this rule.

ESCAPE

The attacker can move any of their models off the battlefield edge labelled 'Escape route' if that model's move is sufficient to take them wholly over the edge of the battlefield. A model that leaves the battlefield this way is not considered to be out of action, but takes no further part in the mission.

BATTLE LENGTH

Use the Variable Battle Length rules (pg 14) – the defender rolls. In addition, if at the end of a battle round all of the attacker's models have escaped (see above) and/or are out of action, the battle ends.

VICTORY CONDITIONS

If, at the end of the battle, more of the attacker's models have escaped than are on the battlefield or have been taken out of action, the attacker wins. Otherwise, the defender wins.

RESOURCES

In a campaign game, if the attacker wins the mission, the defender loses 1 Intelligence and 1 Morale. If the defender wins the mission, the attacker loses 1 Morale.

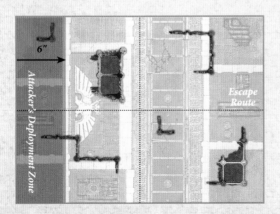

BREAK FREE

Attacker Tactic

Use this Tactic at the beginning of your turn in the Movement phase. Choose a model from your kill team (other than a shaken model) that is within 1" of any enemy models. That model can Advance as if it had not begun the Movement phase within 1" of any enemy models.

1 COMMAND POINT

MATCHED PLAY MISSION
ESCALATING CONFLICT

Your scouts have made contact with the enemy, and are calling in support – they are either pinned in place or have identified an objective that you cannot afford falling into enemy hands. Despatch your finest warriors as quickly as you can to recover your operatives and deny victory to your enemies.

If you are playing a campaign, you can choose to play this mission instead of the Disrupt Supply Lines mission.

THE KILL TEAMS

This is a mission for two to four players. Each player chooses a Faction keyword, and the players reveal their choices at the same time. Then each player chooses a Battle-forged kill team (see the *Kill Team Core Manual*) that only includes models with the Faction keyword they chose. Each kill team can cost up to 125 points.

THE BATTLEFIELD

Create the battlefield and set up terrain. Examples of how you might do this are shown below. Then set up one objective marker in the centre of the battlefield.

SCOUTING PHASE

Resolve the Scouting phase as described in the *Kill Team Core Manual*.

DEPLOYMENT

Each player must divide their kill team into two parts, one of which is approximately half the points value of the other. Players then use the Standard Deployment rules (pg 14) to set up the smaller parts of their kill teams. All other models are automatically set up in Reserve.

BATTLE LENGTH

Use the Variable Battle Length rules (pg 14) – the player with the greatest advantage (determined during deployment) rolls. In addition, if there is only one unbroken kill team on the battlefield at the end of a battle round, the battle ends.

VITAL OBJECTIVE

Models that are within 2" of the centre of the objective marker automatically pass Nerve tests.

VICTORY CONDITIONS

If the battle ends because there is only one unbroken kill team on the battlefield, that kill team's player wins. Otherwise, if one player controls the objective at the end of the battle, that player wins. If no player controls the objective, the player with the greatest Force (in points) on the battlefield (not including shaken models) is the winner. If players are tied for the greatest force, the tied players draw. Any other players lose.

RESOURCES

In a campaign game, the player(s) that lose the mission each lose 1 Intelligence and 1 Materiel. If players draw they do not lose Intelligence or Materiel.

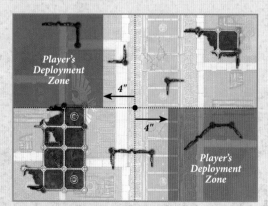

Two-player battlefield using one gameboard

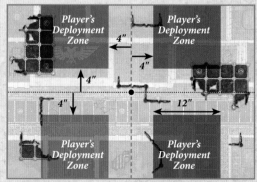

Three- to four-player battlefield using two gameboards

MATCHED PLAY MISSION
CRUSH THEIR CHAMPIONS

Sometimes the simplest solution to a problem is best. Your enemies have proved unbreakable, so with a brazen challenge from your champion, you hope to draw their commanders out, risking your finest warrior for an opportunity to destroy the morale of the opposing armies.

If you are playing a campaign, you can choose to play this mission instead of the Assassinate mission.

THE KILL TEAMS

This is a mission for two to four players. Each player chooses a Faction keyword, and the players reveal their choices at the same time. Then each player chooses a Battle-forged kill team (see the *Kill Team Core Manual*) that only includes models with the Faction keyword they chose. Each kill team can cost up to 200 points and must include one Commander.

THE BATTLEFIELD

Create the battlefield and set up terrain. Examples of how you might do this are shown below.

SCOUTING PHASE

Resolve the Scouting phase as described in the *Kill Team Core Manual*.

DEPLOYMENT

Use the Standard Deployment rules (pg 14). Players cannot set up their Commanders in Reserve.

BATTLE LENGTH

Use the Variable Battle Length rules (pg 14) – the player with the greatest advantage (determined during deployment) rolls.

CRUSHING BLOW

If a player's Commander is out of action when they check to see if their kill team is broken in the Morale phase, their kill team is automatically broken. In addition, whenever a player's Commander takes an enemy model out of action with an attack or psychic power, friendly models within 6" of that Commander that are shaken are no longer shaken.

VICTORY CONDITIONS

If there is only one unbroken kill team on the battlefield at the end of the battle, that kill team's player wins. Otherwise, each player scores 3 victory points for each enemy Commander taken out of action by an attack made or psychic power manifested by a model from their kill team, and 1 victory point for each other enemy specialist taken out of action by an attack made or psychic power manifested by a model from their kill team. The player with the most victory points is the winner. If players are tied for the most victory points, whichever of those players had the lower Force is the winner. If there is still a tie for the most victory points, the tied players draw. Any other players lose.

RESOURCES

In a campaign game, the player(s) that lose the mission each lose 1 Intelligence and 1 Morale. If players draw they do not lose Intelligence or Morale.

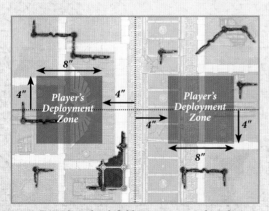

Two-player battlefield using one gameboard

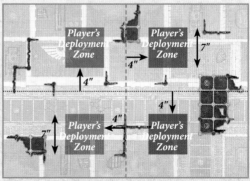

Three- to four-player battlefield using two gameboards

MATCHED PLAY MISSION
OBJECTIVE ULTIMA

A crucial piece of archeotech has become the site of an ongoing battle, as each of the opposing sides struggles to seize it for themselves. As control shifts one way and then the other, it becomes clear that to consolidate their claim, a force also needs to take the surrounding control nodes.

If you are playing a campaign, you can choose to play this mission instead of the Recover Intelligence mission.

THE KILL TEAMS

This is a mission for two to four players. Each player chooses a Faction keyword, and the players reveal their choices at the same time. Then each player chooses a Battle-forged kill team (see the *Kill Team Core Manual*) that only includes models with the Faction keyword they chose. Each kill team can cost up to 125 points.

THE BATTLEFIELD

Create the battlefield and set up terrain. Examples of how you might do this are shown below. Then set up an objective in the centre of the battlefield (this is the primary objective), and four other objectives each halfway between the centre of the battlefield and a corner of the battlefield (these are the secondary objectives).

SCOUTING PHASE

Resolve the Scouting phase as described in the *Kill Team Core Manual*.

DEPLOYMENT

Use the Standard Deployment rules (pg 14).

BATTLE LENGTH

Use the Variable Battle Length rules (pg 14) – the player with the greatest advantage (determined during deployment) rolls.

VICTORY CONDITIONS

If a player controls the primary objective and at least one secondary objective at the end of a battle round, they gain a number of victory points equal to the number of secondary objectives they control. The player with the most victory points at the end of the battle is the winner. If players are tied for the most victory points, whichever of those players controls the primary objective at the end of the battle is the winner. If none of the tied players controls the primary objective, the tied players draw. Any other players lose.

RESOURCES

In a campaign game, the player(s) that lose the mission each lose 1 Intelligence and 1 Territory. If players draw they do not lose Intelligence or Territory.

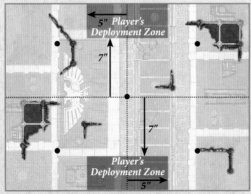

Two-player battlefield using one gameboard

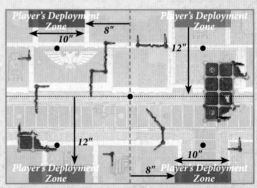

Three- to four-player battlefield using two gameboards

MATCHED PLAY MISSION
SHIFTING PRIORITIES

In the confusion of battle, orders may be garbled or misinterpreted, leaders in the field may prioritise the wrong objective, and fighters can become disoriented. Amidst this maelstrom, a commander with a cool head and the ability to adapt their battle plan on the fly is likely to claim victory.

If you are playing a campaign, you can choose to play this mission instead of the Terror Tactics mission.

THE KILL TEAMS

This is a mission for two to four players. Each player chooses a Faction keyword, and the players reveal their choices at the same time. Then each player chooses a Battle-forged kill team (see the *Kill Team Core Manual*) that only includes models with the Faction keyword they chose. Each kill team can cost up to 200 points and may include a Commander.

THE BATTLEFIELD

Create the battlefield and set up terrain. Examples of how you might do this are shown below. Then set up four objectives each halfway between the centre of the battlefield and a battlefield edge, numbered from 1-4.

SCOUTING PHASE

Resolve the Scouting phase as described in the *Kill Team Core Manual*.

DEPLOYMENT

Use the Standard Deployment rules (pg 14). Models must be set up at least 4" from enemy deployment zones.

BATTLE LENGTH

Use the Variable Battle Length rules (pg 14) – the player with the greatest advantage (determined during deployment) rolls.

PRIORITY ONE

The player with the greatest advantage (determined during deployment) rolls a D6 at the beginning of each battle round, and consults the following table.

D6	RESULT
1	If objective 1 is on the battlefield, remove it from the battlefield.
2	If objective 2 is on the battlefield, remove it from the battlefield.
3	If objective 3 is on the battlefield, remove it from the battlefield.
4	If objective 4 is on the battlefield, remove it from the battlefield.
5-6	If there is no objective in the centre of the battlefield, and any objectives have been removed from the battlefield, set up one of those objectives in the centre of the battlefield.

VICTORY CONDITIONS

Each player scores 1 victory point at the end of each battle round for each objective they control. The player with the most victory points at the end of the battle is the winner. If players are tied for the most victory points, whichever of those players had the lower Force is the winner. If there is still a tie for the most victory points, the tied players draw. Any other players lose.

RESOURCES

In a campaign game, the player(s) that lose the mission each lose 1 Materiel and 1 Territory. If players draw they do not lose Materiel or Territory.

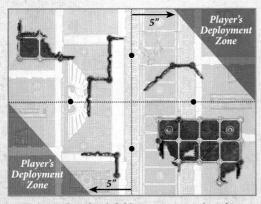

Two-player battlefield using one gameboard

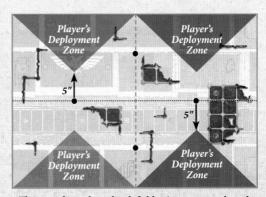

Three- to four-player battlefield using two gameboards

NAME		M	WS	BS	S	T	W	A	Ld	Sv

WEAPON	RANGE	TYPE			S	AP	D	ABILITIES

SUB-FACTION:

ABILITIES:

SPECIALISM: | **DEMEANOUR:**

EXPERIENCE
☐☐☐☐☐☐☐☐☐☐☐☐ **FLESH WOUNDS** ☐☐☐ **CONVALESCENCE** ☐ **NEW RECRUIT** ☐

NAME		M	WS	BS	S	T	W	A	Ld	Sv

WEAPON	RANGE	TYPE			S	AP	D	ABILITIES

SUB-FACTION:

ABILITIES:

SPECIALISM: | **DEMEANOUR:**

EXPERIENCE
☐☐☐☐☐☐☐☐☐☐☐☐ **FLESH WOUNDS** ☐☐☐ **CONVALESCENCE** ☐ **NEW RECRUIT** ☐

NAME		M	WS	BS	S	T	W	A	Ld	Sv

WEAPON	RANGE	TYPE			S	AP	D	ABILITIES

SUB-FACTION:

ABILITIES:

SPECIALISM: | **DEMEANOUR:**

EXPERIENCE
☐☐☐☐☐☐☐☐☐☐☐☐ **FLESH WOUNDS** ☐☐☐ **CONVALESCENCE** ☐ **NEW RECRUIT** ☐

NAME		M	WS	BS	S	T	W	A	Ld	Sv

WEAPON	RANGE	TYPE			S	AP	D	ABILITIES

SUB-FACTION:

ABILITIES:

SPECIALISM: | **DEMEANOUR:**

EXPERIENCE
☐☐☐☐☐☐☐☐☐☐☐☐ **FLESH WOUNDS** ☐☐☐ **CONVALESCENCE** ☐ **NEW RECRUIT** ☐

NAME		M	WS	BS	S	T	W	A	Ld	Sv

WEAPON	RANGE	TYPE			S	AP	D	ABILITIES

SUB-FACTION:

ABILITIES:

SPECIALISM: | **DEMEANOUR:**

LEVEL | **FLESH WOUNDS** ☐☐☐ | **INJURY** | **Contusion** ☐ | **Minor Injury** ☐ | **Serious Injury** ☐

NAME		M	WS	BS	S	T	W	A	Ld	Sv

WEAPON	RANGE	TYPE			S	AP	D	ABILITIES

SUB-FACTION:

ABILITIES:

SPECIALISM: | **DEMEANOUR:**

LEVEL | **FLESH WOUNDS** ☐☐☐ | **INJURY** | **Contusion** ☐ | **Minor Injury** ☐ | **Serious Injur** ☐